STUDY PROJECT ON
SOCIAL RESEARCH
AND DEVELOPMENT
VOLUME 1: Study Project Report

The Federal Investment in Knowledge of Social Problems

Study Project on Social Research and Development
Assembly of Behavioral and Social Sciences
National Research Council

NATIONAL ACADEMY OF SCIENCES
Washington, D.C.   1978

This material is based upon work supported by the National Science Foundation under contract #C-310, Task Order 288. Any opinions, findings, conclusions, or recommendations expressed in this publication are those of the authors and do not necessarily reflect the views of the National Science Foundation.

Library of Congress Cataloging in Publication Data

National Research Council. Study Project on Social Research and Development.
  The Federal investment in knowledge of social problems.

  At head of title: Volume 1, Study Project report.
  Bibliography: p.
  1. Social science research—United States. 2. Policy sciences—United States. 3. Federal aid to research—United States. 4. Evaluation research (Social action programs)—United States. I. Title.
H62.5.U5N38 1978   300′.7′2073   78-7928
ISBN 0-309-02747-0

Available from:
Printing and Publishing Office
National Academy of Sciences
2101 Constitution Avenue, N.W.
Washington, D.C. 20418

Printed in the United States of America

STUDY PROJECT ON SOCIAL RESEARCH AND DEVELOPMENT

This report was prepared by the National Research Council for the National Science Foundation (NSF). At the request of NSF's Science and Technology Policy Office in 1974, the National Research Council agreed to undertake a study of the organization and management of social research and development throughout the federal government. To carry out this task, the Study Project on Social Research and Development was established within the Assembly of Behavioral and Social Sciences of the National Research Council.

The work of the Study Project includes six volumes, to be published in 1978–1979:

Volume 1: *The Federal Investment in Knowledge of Social Problems* (Study Project Report)
Volume 2: *The Funding of Social Knowledge Production and Application: A Survey of Federal Agencies*
Volume 3: *Studies in the Management of Social R&D: Selected Policy Areas*
Volume 4: *Studies in the Management of Social R&D: Selected Issues*
Volume 5: *Knowledge and Policy: The Uncertain Connection*
Volume 6: *The Uses of Basic Research: Case Studies in Social Science*

iv

Contents

Preface

Since this report lays great stress on the importance of knowing your audience, I will begin by saying who we hope will read it. We would be pleased if it were closely read by 43 people who exercise a critical oversight of federal efforts to create and use knowledge of social problems. Let me name them:

The Director of the Office of Management and Budget

The Science and Technology Adviser to the President

The Director of the National Science Foundation and the Chairman of the National Science Board

The Chairman of the U.S. Civil Service Commission

The Secretaries of Health, Education, and Welfare, of Housing and Urban Development, of Labor, and of Transportation

The Chairmen of the Senate and House Appropriations Committees and of their Subcommittees on Housing and Urban Development— Independent Agencies, on Labor, Health, Education, and Welfare, and on Transportation

The Chairmen of the Senate Committee on Banking, Housing and Urban Affairs, of the Committee on Commerce, Science, and Transportation and its Subcommittee on Science, Technology, and Space, of the Committee on Governmental Affairs, and of the Committee on

Human Resources and its Subcommittees on Health and Scientific Research, on Aging, on Alcoholism and Drug Abuse, on Child and Human Development, on Education, Arts, and Humanities, on Employment, Poverty, and Migratory Labor, on the Handicapped, and on Labor

The Chairmen of the House Committee on Banking, Finance and Urban Affairs, of the Committee on Education and Labor and its Subcommittees on Compensation, Health, and Safety, on Economic Opportunity, on Employment Opportunities, on Elementary, Secondary, and Vocational Education, on Postsecondary Education, on Select Education, on Labor-Management Relations, and on Labor Standards, of the Committee on Government Operations, and of the Committee on Science and Technology and its Subcommittees on Domestic and International Scientific Planning, Analysis, and Cooperation and on Science, Research and Technology

The Comptroller General of the United States

The Assistant Secretary for Planning and Evaluation of the Department of Health, Education, and Welfare, the Assistant Secretary for Policy Development and Research of the Department of Housing and Urban Development, and the Assistant Secretary for Policy, Evaluation, and Research of the Department of Labor.

We would be well satisfied if our analysis reached only this critically important oversight group—but we want and expect to reach a wider audience as well. This report is meant to help those who administer the system of federal support for the production and application of knowledge of social problems. Some of our ideas are directed to those who manage federal programs of support for social research and development (R&D); some to those in the Congress and the executive branch who help to shape federal policy on social R&D; and some to all those in the government, the research community, and the nation at large who want to see knowledge brought effectively to bear on social problems.

The Study Project on Social Research and Development grew out of concerns of federal officials responsible for both science policy and social policy. It was commissioned by the Science and Technology Policy Office, then the staff arm of the director of the National Science Foundation in his role as science adviser to the President. The director and officials in the Science and Technology Policy Office were concerned about the limited information available to the government on the scope of programs of social research and development, the lack of consistency in policies for managing research programs, and the lack of understanding of the impact on the research community of the decisions made by the managers of these programs. These concerns were shared by officials in the Office of Management and Budget and in several other executive departments and agencies. As a result, the National Academy of Sciences was asked to survey the size and location of budgetary support for social research and development throughout the executive branch. Subsequently, the Academy was asked to broaden its study to recommend ways in which the federal government could more effectively develop and apply knowledge about social problems.

The need to develop a comprehensive view of the present system of social research and development was plain from the varied diagnoses of what is wrong with it. We found a remarkable range of ideas as to where the problem lies.

Some of these locate the difficulty within the policy-making arms of government. It is said that the time perspectives of policy makers are excessively short; that they cannot free themselves from urgent matters of the moment to deal with the important longer-term problems facing the country; that they cannot conscientiously seek out available information on social problems; that they rarely understand the process of research or surround themselves with those who do; that they bend research and development to political ends; that they defend the turfs of their particular agencies or committees, with too little regard for the need to coordinate the planning and use of research across units of the government with interdependent functions.

Others locate the difficulty in those officials in the government who are responsible for managing the funding of social research and development. It is said that these managers do not plan effectively; that they use the wrong instruments to support research work; that they pay too little attention to quality; that they have unrealistic ideas of what can be accomplished by research in a given amount of time; that they are preoccupied by new starts and individual projects and fail to accumulate the knowledge that can be gained from a series of projects; that they devote too little attention to disseminating the results of the research they support.

Still other diagnoses locate the difficulty in the research community. It is said that research performers resist being held to account; that to obtain funding they promise results they cannot deliver; that they adapt their results to the sponsor's biases; that the for-profit performers, despite islands of excellence, have flooded the market with shoddy work as they pursue new contracts; that the universities have been unwilling to create the institutions and the faculty incentives that would turn disciplinary knowledge toward social needs.

Although there is a kernel of truth in most of these assertions, their varied content argues the need to see the system whole. The body of this report describes the steps we took to develop a more comprehensive view.

This report is one of a number published over the past decade that deal with specific facets of social research and its use. Each is a product of its time and of the aspirations social scientists then held. It is useful to characterize these earlier efforts, even if selectively, to better appreciate the background and climate in which our study was undertaken.

The Behavioral Sciences in the Federal Government (Young Report) was published by the National Academy of Sciences in 1968. It was primarily concerned with means of improving the use of social research by agencies of the federal government in making federal policy. The deliberations of the Young committee took place before an assessment could be made of the impact of the significant increase in expenditures for social research that accompanied the programs of the Great Society. The committee sought to improve the capacity of the government to commission and use social research by recommending that more trained social scientists be hired by federal agencies and that the representation of the social science community on the President's Science Advisory Committee (PSAC) and in the Office of Science and Technology be enlarged. It also recommended that an independent National Institute for Advanced Research and Public Policy be endowed by the government to conduct interdisciplinary and future-oriented research.

In 1969 the Academy and the Social Science Research Council published *The Behavioral and Social Sciences: Outlook and Needs* (BASS Report). This report was one of a series that assessed the status and needs of various scientific disciplines, and a number of discipline-specific volumes were issued. There was also a central report, which asserted that federal support for the behavioral and social sciences should increase at the rate of 12 to 18 percent per year on the ground that the normal growth of the social and behavioral science community, as well as social need, justified it. Beyond this, the report echoed the Young committee's call for improved representation on PSAC, proposed the development of improved and interlinked data bases, stressed the importance of providing for the training of social and behavioral scientists, and proposed the creation of a system of social indicators. It also suggested that social and behavioral scientists outside the government issue an annual social report to the nation. The report recognized that discipline-centered work frequently was unable to grapple with social problems and proposed that funds be provided to create a number of graduate schools of applied behavioral science.

At about the same time, the Special Commission on the Social Sciences of the National Science Board published *Knowledge into Action: Improving the Nation's Use of the Social Sciences* (Brim Report). This report was concerned with improving the use of social science research and called for better social science training for the professions, employment of individuals with social science training in key government positions, improved data bases, and better understanding of social science by labor, community organizations, and the public. The Brim Report also recommended the continued presence of social scientists on PSAC and the presence of social scientists other than economists on the staff of the Council of Economic Advisers. The report also recognized the limitations of disciplinary approaches to social problems. In view of the pervasive disciplinary organization of universities, it called for the establishment of problem-centered institutes of social research, which might be independent of universities.

Most of these reports were written from a disciplinary perspective. Each included recommendations that could easily appear self-serving to critics of social research even if they were not. None looked deeply into the motives of the government for supporting research or into the limitations of applying the results of social research in the policy process. The discussions of use dealt almost entirely with federal officials, although the Brim Report did consider nonfederal audiences.

Four reports of quite a different nature, which relate to our task, have appeared recently. Each of them was published by the National Academy of Sciences. *Knowledge and Policy in Manpower: A Study of the Manpower Research and Development Program in the Department of Labor* examined the programs of the Office of Manpower Research and Development in the Department of Labor; *Social and Behavioral Science Programs in the National Science Foundation* evaluated the quality of those programs within the National Science Foundation; *Assessing Vocational Education Research and Development* evaluated the programs of vocational education research and development supported by the Office of Education of the Department of Health, Education, and Welfare; *Understanding Crime: An Evaluation of the National Institute of Law Enforcement and Criminal Justice* focused on the research program of the Law Enforcement Assistance Administration of the Department of Justice. Collectively, these reports differed from the earlier ones in that they were based on evaluations of selected federal programs of social knowledge production and application. Each examined the nature of the management processes in the agencies in question. Each was critical of some aspects of the way in which research is commissioned, funds allocated, and research monitored. Each provided some guidance as to the research issues that need attention.

Our study differs from these earlier studies in several respects. Both this report and the supporting studies devote considerable attention to describing the nature of the policy process itself in order to provide a more realistic basis for assessing the contribution that can be made by social knowledge. Concern for the policy process led the Study Project to stress the limitations of social research as a tool for making social policy or for operating social programs. The earlier reports hinted at these limitations, but few addressed directly their implications for the federal role in social R&D.

This study encompasses all government agencies that commission and fund social research and deals with some general problems of the system of federal support. In this sense, it extends across the whole of the government the concerns of the committees that examined the performance of individual agencies. We are therefore able to ask how well the entire complex of agencies funding social knowledge production and application fits together, what problems these agencies seem to share, and whether there are modifications of government policy that would benefit the system as a whole. The scope of the study permitted us to take a portfolio view of the federal investment in social research and development.

This report focuses on several issues that were largely ignored in the earlier reports. We have, for example, traced the implications of the fact that more than half of all federally supported social knowledge production and application is meant to benefit policy makers and others outside the federal government; past studies paid little attention to the needs of these nonfederal users. We also give sustained attention to program activities intended to support the application as opposed to the production of knowledge. This subject has attracted an extensive literature but is often neglected by those concerned with federal science policy.

Our study has been a collaborative venture, and our debts are many. Henry David, near the end of his long service as executive director of the Assembly of Behavioral and Social Sciences, and the Executive Committee of the Assembly organized our committee and launched its work. David A. Goslin, his successor as executive director, has unfailingly supported our efforts, as has Lester P. Silverman, the associate executive director. Robert McC. Adams, the chairman of the Executive Committee when we began our work, gave the project critical intellectual support and was a member of the committee until he withdrew to pursue his research in the Middle East. Ernest F. Powers of the Science and Technology Policy Office was intimately involved in defining the objectives of the study and has supplied throughout a gifted R&D manager's blend of encouragement and concern for deadlines. Vincent P. Rock organized our staff work as executive secretary and oversaw the preliminary data collection for our survey of federal expenditures before he was lured away to become staff director of a study of the United States Senate.

We owe a very great deal to Thomas K. Glennan, Jr., who served as study director for virtually the whole period of our research. He has left his mark on this report and the analyses on which it draws at many points. Laurence E. Lynn, Jr., a member of the committee with broad experience in government, took direct responsibility for our studies of the management of social research and development in four selected policy areas. Among those who worked in some capacity with Glennan and Lynn we owe a particular debt to Mark A. Abramson, who was by the end the master shepherd of our survey of federal expenditures and is responsible for the Appendix to this volume and the separate report on the survey; and to Cheryl D. Hayes, who did a path-breaking analysis of demonstration projects and has creatively joined in our writing efforts at innumerable points. Beyond this the committee is deeply grateful for the work of Eugenia Grohman, our gifted editor, as well as of the many staff members, consultants, and interns who participated in the work of the project. Christine L. Davis and Linda Ingram were staff members who wrote important background papers for the Study Project. Sharon M. Collins, Richard Collins Davis, and John M. Seidl served as consultants and also wrote papers that are now part of this report's companion volumes.

Vincent Rock directed the first data collection efforts, and Arthur L. Canfield, Benjamin Caplan, John Grady, Linda Ingram, Jeremiah Norris, Rita O'Connor, Howard Simons, and Richard C. Taeuber served as interviewers. Mark Abramson directed the 1976 data collection, which became the basis for our survey, and Bruce Craig, Patricia P. Koshel, John McCann, Joshua Minkove, Pamela Neff, Jeffrey Nesvet, Diane Rothberg, Howard Simons, and Jan Solomon served as interviewers. We are indebted to Patricia Koshel for supervising the collection of data from agencies of the Department of Health, Education, and Welfare and to Jan Solomon for the computer work on the 1976 survey data. Jill Klaskin, the committee's administrative secretary, has kept us generally in order with great efficiency and also served as administrative assistant for the survey. Rose Gunn and Susan Hegedus provided excellent secretarial support; extraordinary typing efforts were also contributed by Marcie Hazard and Karen Kellerhouse.

This report too is a collaborative venture. Thomas Glennan prepared the ground with several background drafts. The integrative pieces written by Laurence Lynn for our companion volumes on policy relevance and the management of social R&D were also important background materials, and Lynn made pivotal contributions to our final text. But every member of the committee has shaped our report, and responsibility for our analysis and recommendations rests with the committee as a whole.

Donald E. Stokes, *Chairman*
Study Project on
Social Research and Development

Summary

The federal government invests nearly $2 billion a year to acquire and use knowledge of social problems. This figure is small when compared to the cost of research and development outside the social fields and minuscule when compared to the cost of operating the government's social programs. But it is three times larger in real terms than it was in the early 1960s, and quite large enough to invite the attention of those who are concerned about the federal investment in knowledge of social problems. This report probes the nature of this investment—its scale, its management, and the return the nation needs from it—and considers how the present system of federal support might be strengthened.

The concepts we use to define our subject are in one respect novel. We replace the conventional idea of social "research and development" with a concept of social "knowledge production and application" that gives a sharper description of federal efforts to acquire and use knowledge of social problems. This concept embraces four types of *knowledge production*—research on social problems, the collection of social statistics, evaluations of social programs, and demonstration projects aiding the formation of social policy—and three of *knowledge application*—demonstration projects aiding the implementation of social policy, the development of materials related to social problems, and efforts to synthesize, disseminate, or use knowledge of social problems.

We have viewed this system of activities from several analytical perspectives, with the aid of several background studies.

1

- A new analysis of the federal budget and extensive interviews in the federal agencies disclosed the scale and pattern of federal investment in social knowledge production and application (*The Funding of Social Knowledge Production and Application: A Survey of Federal Agencies* [Abramson 1978]).
- Case studies of knowledge production and application activities on health, income security, the enhancement of the living environment, and development in early childhood provided a view of management in selected policy areas (*Studies in the Management of Social R&D: Selected Policy Areas* [Lynn 1978b]).
- Studies of staffing, instruments of support, and the role of demonstrations provided better insight into the problems of managing the federal investment (*Studies in the Management of Social R&D: Selected Issues* [Glennan 1978]).
- New analyses by observers familiar with government and the research community helped to illuminate the relationship between knowledge and policy (*Knowledge and Policy: The Uncertain Connection* [Lynn 1978a]).
- Special studies of the rise of a new field of knowledge (demography), the development of a new methodology (survey research), and the antecedents of a new policy option (the negative income tax) explored the return on the nation's investment in basic advances in social science (*The Uses of Basic Research: Case Studies in Social Science* [Stokes 1978]).

We set forth in this main report our key findings about the present system of support, our conclusions about the problem of organizing and managing the federal investment, and our recommendations about how the system might be strengthened.

FINDINGS

Our analysis of budget obligations examined four patterns in federal support for social knowledge production and application.

- The pattern by *type of activity* is far more varied than the conventional idea of social research and development might suggest. Activities that are in a strict sense research claim about one-third of total expenditures for the production and use of knowledge of social problems. All types of knowledge production account for two-thirds of the total; all types of knowledge application, for one-third.

- The pattern by *policy area* shows that 60 percent of all support is related to human resources, with 28 percent related to community resources and the remaining 12 percent related to natural resources and the science and technology base. The allocation of support between production and application of knowledge varies widely across policy areas. For all areas, the amount spent on social knowledge production and application totals no more than six-tenths of one percent (0.006) of the amount spent on social programs.
- The pattern by *organizational location* shows that funding programs are strongly decentralized, with 180 separate agencies supporting knowledge production and application activities. Of the total amount spent, more than one-half is channeled through program-operating agencies and the rest through departmental policy offices, independent R&D agencies, and specialized statistical agencies.
- The pattern by *audience* shows that those who are meant to benefit from social knowledge production and application activities lie to a remarkable extent outside the federal government. The amount spent on activities directed to nonfederal users exceeds the amount spent on activities directed to federal users by more than two to one, and this ratio is still higher for spending by the mission (operating) agencies.

Our studies of the operation of the system led us to a series of findings about the way research agendas are set, knowledge is applied, and the system is managed.

- The *setting of research agendas* is largely a reactive process, with few examples of systematic planning. The incentives for planning are weak and inconsistent. Although there is little duplication of research effort, there is also little coordinated planning among agencies. Hence, there are important problems that fall in the gaps between agencies, and little attention is given to identifying and planning research on emerging problems that are not well matched to the existing responsibilities of mission agencies.
- Effective *application of knowledge* is hampered by doubts as to the quality or relevance of the results of research and other knowledge production activities, by the lack of clear policies on the dissemination and use of results, and by a weak sense of the appropriate audience for many results. An excessive focus on individual projects discourages efforts to synthesize and cumulate results. Research administrators have limited understanding of how new information fosters innovation and change.

• The *management of the system* is handicapped by the rapid turnover of leadership at the highest level of government and by arbitrary staff ceilings and unresponsive hiring policies for support agencies. Uncertainties of funding are a pervasive problem, with harm resulting from unforeseen prosperity as well as from unscheduled poverty. The selection among alternative methods of support rarely reflects a clear conception of how research planning and problem choice should be shared between funding agencies and those performing the funded work.

CONCLUSIONS

Our account of the existing system of support shows that the federal government in effect holds a diversified portfolio of investments in knowledge of social problems. Its varied investments yield different types of return and require different policies for effective management. The diversity of the portfolio can be described in terms of the lapse of time and complexity of the links between investment and return.

• *Program-supporting* activities offer information to meet the short-run, limited, and well-specified requirements of operating social programs.

• *Policy-forming* activities offer information that may help in making social policy in the somewhat longer run.

• *Problem-exploring* activities offer a deeper understanding of social problems that may help to define future policy options, even if no specific program or policy needs were initially in view.

• *Knowledge-building* activities enlarge the resources of social knowledge or method, with applications to the understanding of social problems, the forming of social policy, or the operation of social programs that are varied, difficult to forecast, and typically long run.

The need for diversified investment is closely linked to three pervasive characteristics of government—its political character, its need to act on incomplete information, and its brief time perspective.

• The *political character of government* means that the production and use of knowledge needs effective political support, but a political constituency is more easily found for some parts of the federal portfolio than for others. In particular, political support for longer-term, more speculative investments of high potential return is a continuing problem of the system.

- The *need of government to act on incomplete information* highlights the fact that research can make only a partial input and is, in any period, a limited and potentially costly resource. Hence, the federal investment in research should direct it where it will count for most.
- The *brief time perspective of government* means that some knowledge production and application must serve short-run event-forced needs of government. But the longer life span of major social problems allows for a significant return from research that requires a longer time perspective. Effective management of the federal investment should provide for both of these perspectives.

RECOMMENDATIONS

In view of the inherent diversity of the system, we avoid sweeping organizational prescriptions. Informed oversight of the system by those in Congress and the executive branch who have cross-cutting responsibilities can help to create the incentives for needed change. We offer a series of recommendations for improving the way research agendas are set, knowledge is applied, and the system is managed.

Our principal recommendations for improving the setting of research agendas are these:

- Federal research administrators and oversight officials should devote more resources to developing systematic planning as a distinct aspect of efforts to produce and use knowledge of social problems.
- Program decision makers should have greater input into the planning of program-supporting research and policy makers at the departmental and presidential levels and in Congress should have greater input into the planning of policy-forming research.
- Special attention should be given to building problem-exploring research agendas through task forces and conferences and the creation of presidential or joint presidential-congressional temporary commissions.
- A number of problem-centered research programs should be created to undertake intensive and sustained work on major social problems.
- More adequate methods should be developed for forecasting new or emerging social problems and creating research agendas directed to them.
- Users of research-based knowledge outside the government should be more closely involved in establishing priorities for research that is meant to benefit them.
- Scientific criteria, rather than problem or policy relevance, should

guide the setting of priorities for research that seeks to enlarge the general resources of social knowledge or method.

Our principal recommendations for improving the dissemination and application of knowledge are these:

- Oversight agencies and research administrators should give more attention to the dissemination of high-quality research results to appropriate audiences.
- Federal agencies supporting social knowledge production and application should sponsor periodic syntheses of the knowledge gained from the research they fund.
- More intensive research on the process of social change and the adoption of innovations by federal and nonfederal policy makers should be undertaken by agencies supporting social knowledge production and application.

Our principal recommendations for improving the management of the system are these:

- Appropriate oversight agencies should regularly review the allocation of social knowledge production and application resources among policy areas, organizations, and categories of activities within their jurisdictions.
- Oversight agencies should periodically review the staffing and funding of agencies supporting social knowledge production and application and tailor the capabilities of these agencies to their missions and responsibilities.
- Departments and agencies should organize their planning and budgeting activities to provide a significant role for knowledge brokers, who should assume increased responsibility for policy planning and program development.
- Each agency should review its grant and contract policies to increase its awareness of available options and to base its choice among alternative instruments of support on a clear view of how responsibility for research planning and problem choice should be shared between the agency and the research performer.
- Departmental planning, policy analysis, and evaluation offices should promote periodic evaluations by knowledge-production agencies of the work they fund, with priority given to the largest and most important programs of support.

1 Introduction

In recent years the federal government has increased its investment in research on social problems and has relied more heavily on staff trained in the social and behavioral sciences. During fiscal 1977 the government spent more than $1.8 billion to collect social statistics, support social research and development, carry out demonstrations, evaluate social programs and policies, and disseminate information about these activities. Although the research and development portion of this total is only four percent of federal expenditures for all research and development (R&D), it has roughly tripled in real terms since the early 1960s.[1] Moreover, there are now several thousand employees in positions in the federal service for which social and behavioral science training is required, and even larger numbers of professional social scientists hold policy-making positions in the executive agencies, in Congress, and even in the judiciary.

But these trends are matched by rising dissatisfaction in some quarters. For a variety of reasons—some valid, some not—the social R&D community has come under increasing pressure to give an accounting of its usefulness to policy makers, program officials, and legislators. Unquestionably, an activity this large contains inefficient, even pernicious, elements along with elements so valuable that to curtail them would be unthinkable. For some critics, however, the

[1]Henry David, "Two Transformations: Aspects of Social, Economic, and Science Policies in Twentieth Century America," hereafter cited as David, "Two Transformations," *in* Stokes (1978).

concern for accountability reflects frustration with the failure of social programs to achieve their goals and the belief that the experts in the research community are at least partially to blame. Others, including many federal executives with social science backgrounds, simply believe that the payoffs in useful knowledge from investments in social R&D have been too small.

Whatever the reason, the pressures for relevance have taken the tangible form of a significant tightening up of federal management of social R&D: increasing reliance on competitively awarded contracts instead of grants and on grant arrangements that involve collaboration between grantor and grantee; pressures from management and budget personnel to improve contract and grant administration and research monitoring, dissemination and utilization; increasing skepticism about the use of peer review panels and research-community-oriented advisory councils; and a greater stress on the forms of social R&D that seem most useful to policy makers—program evaluation, policy analysis, expert consultation, and social experimentation—relative to traditional social science research performed at universities. Indeed, a major charge to this committee by its sponsor was to recommend specific ways of improving the policy relevance of federally supported social R&D.

There is no evidence that these measures have improved the quality and value of social R&D. Attempts at reform may actually have made matters worse by enmeshing research administrators and investigators in a regulatory process that inhibits rather than facilitates the quality, timeliness, and applicability of social R&D. There is the prospect of a vicious cycle: federal attempts to improve accountability through tighter management may produce disappointing results and lead to still further controls and further frustration on every side.

The cycle should be broken. The social problems facing the nation will be difficult and complex in the years ahead. Every part of the government, and many of the organizations and individuals served by the government, will need better information on what the problems are, how they may be solved, and at what cost. Although judgment and practical wisdom will continue to be the most important ingredients of decision making, systematic research will become an increasingly important source of insights, ideas, and evidence. Under these circumstances, resistance by policy makers to investing in and applying new knowledge will be detrimental both to the development of effective governmental policies and to the maintenance of the creative energies of the research community.

THE FOCUS OF THE STUDY

What can be done to improve the current system of federal support for social research and development? How can federal expenditures on social R&D more effectively meet the needs of society? This report is intended to help answer these questions. To do so, we first describe the programs through which the federal government supports the production and application of knowledge of social problems; this funding system is our immediate focus.

This report concerns the ways in which the federal government gains and applies knowledge of social problems through its support of (a) knowledge-producing activities, including research, statistical reporting, program evaluations, and policy-formulating demonstrations that bear on social problems; and of (b) knowledge-applying activities, including policy-implementing demonstrations, the development of materials, and other methods of synthesizing, disseminating, and using knowledge of social problems. Definitions of these activities are presented on the following two pages.

As noted, four of our seven categories of activities fall outside the scope of social R&D as traditionally defined. The additional types of activities are an integral part of the effort of the government to promote the creation and use of knowledge of social problems and seemed to us a proper part of our study. Moreover, the term "development," which is well understood when applied, for example, to military weapons systems, often is without a parallel in the social sphere. We will therefore consistently prefer our broader conceptualization of "social knowledge production and application," although we will not banish the term "social R&D" from these pages.[2]

There is a hazy boundary between what is social and what is not. We have thought of "social" as referring to the behavior of individuals, groups, or institutions. Such a definition excludes biomedical or technological projects in which only minor attention is given to social or individual impacts; it would include a project assessing the impact of an existing technological capability on behavior. This is a difficult line to draw and we will note several areas in which the distinction between social and nonsocial activities remains a matter of judgment.

Although the immediate focus of our study is federal support for activities that fall within this definition of social knowledge production

---

[2]The Appendix gives a more detailed discussion of the similarities and differences between a traditional R&D framework and our framework.

DEFINITION OF SOCIAL KNOWLEDGE PRODUCTION AND KNOWLEDGE APPLICATION ACTIVITIES

Knowledge Production

Research Research is systematic, intensive study directed toward greater knowledge or understanding of the subject studied. Social research includes basic, applied, or policy research that studies either the behavior of individuals, groups, or institutions or the effects of policies, programs, or technologies on behavior.†

Demonstrations for Policy Formulation A demonstration is a small-scale program undertaken in an operational setting for a finite period of time to test the desirability of a proposed course of action. A demonstration for policy formulation is undertaken to learn new information about the outcomes and administrative feasibility of a proposed action. Social experiments are included in this category.

*Program Evaluation Program evaluation is evaluation that seeks to systematically analyze federal programs (or their components) to determine the extent to which they have achieved their objectives. A distinguishing factor of program evaluation is that national operating programs (or their components) are evaluated for the use of agency decision makers in making policy or program decisions. Program evaluation is defined as a management tool; more general types of evaluation studies (activities frequently labeled evaluation research) were judged not to be oriented to management or decision making and were categorized as research.†

*General Purpose Statistics General purpose statistics include either current or periodic data of general interest and use. A characteristic of general purpose statistics is that many of the specific users and uses are unknown. These statistics provide all levels of government and the private sector with information on a very broad spectrum of social, economic, and demographic topics. Statistics that are collected for the specific purpose of providing research data in a specific area of inquiry have been categorized as research.†

Knowledge Application

*Demonstrations for Policy Implementation   A demonstration is a small-scale program undertaken in an operational setting for a finite period of time to test the desirability of a proposed course of action. A demonstration for policy implementation is undertaken to promote the use of a particular action. This type of demonstration does not attempt to generate new information but instead attempts to apply existing knowledge.

Development of Materials   The development of materials consists of the systematic use of knowledge and understanding gained from research to produce materials. Examples of such materials are educational curriculum materials or methods, testing instruments, and management or training curricula. Such materials are used in a variety of educational, training, or testing settings.†

*Dissemination   Dissemination consists of activities undertaken by research managers or others to promote the application of knowledge or data resulting from social knowledge production activities.† Dissemination activities include:

Publication and distribution of scientific and technical information resulting from social research;

Documentation, reference, and information services (information retrieval systems);

Research syntheses written for the use of practitioners and decision makers;

Technical assistance to practitioners to disseminate knowledge;

Support of conferences to disseminate information; and

Creation of dissemination networks and consortia.

---

*The asterisked categories fall outside the definition of research and development used by the National Science Foundation and the Office of Management and Budget. This knowledge production and knowledge application framework can thus be viewed as containing social R&D and related activities.

†These definitions are similar to those used by the National Science Foundation and the Office of Management and Budget. For a fuller discussion of these definitions, see the Appendix.

11

and application, we could hardly do justice to our subject without looking beyond these funding programs. Consider utilization: the ways that knowledge of social problems is used in making federal policy or operating federal programs reach far beyond the explicitly funded efforts to apply knowledge that are included in our definition of knowledge-application activities. Indeed, few of the steps by which Congress and federal agencies translate knowledge into social policy are separately budgeted and accounted for in this way. Furthermore, although the federal government is the world's leading investor in research on social problems, a variety of other public and private sources in this country and abroad help to create the knowledge the nation uses in facing its social problems. This wider view emphasizes the fact that the objective in applying knowledge should be to use effectively information from all sources and not just to be sure that the knowledge paid for by the federal government is somehow disseminated and used.

At times the users of knowledge also lie outside the federal government. Indeed, the majority of research funded by the federal government is intended for use not by Congress or federal agencies but by state and local governments, school systems, hospitals, police forces, industry, and the public at large. We refer to these potential users as "third parties"—federal sponsors and research performers being the "first" and "second" parties. Issues surrounding the effective use of "third-party" research are a main concern of this report.

The following chart summarizes the categorization of those who fund the production of knowledge of social problems and those who use that knowledge:

Knowledge Is Used

Knowledge Is Produced	Within the Federal Government	Outside the Federal Government
With Federal Funding	a	b
With Other Funding	c	d

Much of our analysis centers on activities in cell *a* of the chart: the federal government pays the bill and is the primary audience of the knowledge that results. For example, the Office of the Assistant Secretary for Planning and Evaluation in the Department of Health, Education, and Welfare (HEW) may fund studies of the availability and utilization of health services among low-income populations and use the results to help design a national health insurance policy. But our analysis also concerns activities in cell *b* of the chart: the federal government funds work that is addressed to the needs of third parties. For example, the Division of Community Development and Management in the Department of Housing and Urban Development (HUD) may support studies of ways that state and local governments can improve the productivity of their delivery of social services. Moreover, we are concerned with the effectiveness of activities in cell *c* of the chart: the key issue is the effectiveness with which the government identifies and uses knowledge created without federal support. The federal government might, for example, use the results of foundation-supported studies of public financing of national election campaigns. Only the knowledge of social problems not supported with federal funds or used by the federal government—activities in cell *d* of the chart—is beyond the scope of our study.

We see federal support for social knowledge production and application as part of a wider process by which the nation produces and uses knowledge of social problems. We did not come to this view all at once at the beginning of our work. On the contrary, we built up by stages a framework for looking at this broader process, and this framework is one of the products of our work.

THE PLAN OF THE STUDY

It was clear from the outset that we would need to gather a wide range of information. Our resources for doing so were modest. Measured against either the scope of the subject or the funds often made available to national commissions, ours was a small study, but we have tried to gain a better, empirically based understanding of social R&D. The groundwork for this report is a set of analytical studies by staff and consultants with varied types of expertise. These studies are published in a series of companion volumes to this report and are a main outcome of our work.

Since we were asked to examine the federal support of social R&D, we undertook first a survey of dollar obligations for social knowledge production and application across all federal agencies.[3] After consulting with budget officials in each of the agencies, we developed a new classification of these obligations, which we initially applied to the budget for fiscal 1975. We then refined the classification and repeated the survey nearly two years later to obtain comparable figures for fiscal 1976 and fiscal 1977. These data are presented in Chapter 2 of this report, which describes the scope of the federal investment in social knowledge production and application, the policy areas on which it is focused, the agencies in which it is located, and the users for whom its results are intended. A brief account of the technical aspects of these surveys appears in the Appendix; a more comprehensive report of the figures for the major departments and agencies is published as a separate volume, *The Funding of Social Knowledge Production and Application: A Survey of Federal Agencies* (Abramson 1978).

A second effort of our study focused on the way the federal government manages its investment in social knowledge production and application in four selected problem areas: health, income security, the living environment, and early childhood development. The interviews in each area probed the way in which research agendas are set, the effectiveness of alternative instruments of support, the importance of continuity in funding, the nature of interagency relationships, the role of knowledge brokers, the influence of users and sponsors, and the dissemination of research results. We draw extensively on these studies in Chapter 3 of this report, and they comprise another volume in the series, *Studies in the Management of Social R&D: Selected Policy Areas* (Lynn 1978b).

A third group of studies assessed experience on four management issues: planning; the use of grants and contracts in supporting research, a subject that was explored in a special conference of R&D program managers and grant and procurement officers from a number of federal agencies; uses and examples of "demonstrations"; and staffing patterns in eight agencies that are heavily involved in social research and development. The last study examines in particular the relationship between the size of funding programs and the availability of staff. We draw on these studies too in Chapter 3 of this report, and they comprise another volume in the series, *Studies in the Management of Social R&D: Selected Issues* (Glennan 1978).

In the course of the project we commissioned two other kinds of analyses to explore the wider context of the funding of social R&D. One centered on the elusive concept of "policy relevance." It was

---

[3]Although the general terms "expenditure" and "spending" are used throughout the report, our survey was actually based on budget obligations.

clear that this was an influential concept in current debates about the role of social research and development, but it was also clear that the concept needed more clarity. We therefore invited papers from a group of observers of broad experience with both social research and social policy. These have contributed to Chapter 4 of this report and have elsewhere shaped our thinking on a number of points. They too are published as a volume in the series, *Knowledge and Policy: The Uncertain Connection* (Lynn 1978a).

The final group of analyses dealt with how the investment in basic advances in social knowledge and method might strengthen the nation's capacity to deal with social problems. We commissioned for this purpose a historical review of the federal role in creating and using social knowledge and three analytical case histories of basic advances in the social and behavioral sciences. One, a study of the rise of modern demography, explored the return from the investment in a major new field of knowledge. Another, a study of the development of survey research, explored the return from the investment in a major new research methodology. The third, a study of the social science bases of negative income tax proposals, explored the theoretical and methodological antecedents of a major new option of social policy.[4] They have also helped shape the views we set out in Chapter 4 of this report, and they comprise the last of our series of companion volumes, *The Uses of Basic Research: Case Studies in Social Science* (Stokes 1978).

Chapters 2 and 3 describe the current system of federal support for social knowledge production and application, drawing on our surveys of budget obligations and our analyses of management practice. But we derived more than a descriptive account of the existing system from these studies; we came to see more clearly the variety of federal investments in social knowledge production and application and also some pervasive difficulties in linking research to policy.

Following from this, Chapter 4 explores three characteristics of government that weaken its thrust toward an effective, research-based understanding of social problems. In Chapter 4 we also suggest the benefit to be gained by taking a portfolio approach to investments in research, expecting a very different return from different types of investment and matching very different policies on support and utilization to each. Chapter 5, using the information and insights of Chapters 2 and 3 and the perspectives of Chapter 4, recommends how the system of social knowledge production and application might be improved.

[4]The analytical case histories were jointly sponsored by the Study Project and a panel of the Advisory Committee on Research of the National Science Foundation under a special grant from the Foundation.

2 Federal Spending for Social Knowledge Production and Application

Federal expenditures for social R&D have grown rapidly over the past decade, particularly with the advent of the new social programs. The Office of Management and Budget (OMB) and the staff of the science and technology adviser to the President have tracked these expenditures as part of the special analysis of R&D items in the federal budget. But a great deal more can be learned about the recent pattern of federal support for social knowledge production and application by classifying these expenditures in several new ways.

Our survey examined some 180 agencies[1] in 44 organizational entities that support identifiable amounts of knowledge production and application in 12 social policy areas. We identified the distinct programs of funding for social knowledge production and application within each of these agencies and then classified these programs in ways that reflected our analytical objectives. This method required extensive interviewing within the departments and agencies in addition to inspecting budget data.

We developed four classifications. The first is by type of activity, as defined in Chapter 1; the second is by policy area; the third is by type and organizational location of the funding agency; and the fourth is by the objective or audience of the activity being supported. This chapter

[1]The term "agency" refers to any organizational unit of a cabinet-level department (including bureaus, divisions, offices, and services) or any independent organizational unit, other than a cabinet-level department, whose principal officer reports directly to the President.

16

examines the data by applying these classifications singly and in combination.[2]

FUNDING PATTERNS BY TYPE OF ACTIVITY

The level of federal funding for fiscal 1976 for each type of social knowledge production and application activity is presented in Table 1. It is noteworthy that two-thirds of all obligations in that year were for knowledge production and one-third for application. The largest category of spending was research, including basic, applied, and policy research, which accounted for more than one-third of all obligations. However, the substantial obligations for policy formulation demonstrations, for program evaluations, and for general purpose statistics suggest the importance of other means by which the federal government invests in the production of knowledge of social problems.

Table 1 also reveals that the two categories of demonstration projects accounted for almost one-fifth of all obligations for social knowledge production and application. The support of demonstrations as a means of gaining new knowledge, as well as of applying knowledge, has received far too little attention. The figures show that federal obligations for demonstrations were divided roughly evenly between projects that sought new information (demonstrations for policy formulation) and projects that promoted the adoption of a program (demonstrations for policy implementation). These figures exclude a third type of spending, for operating programs masquerading as "demonstrations," where the objective is neither to gain nor to disseminate knowledge.[3]

Table 1 shows that almost $600 million was obligated by the federal government to knowledge application activities in fiscal 1976. Except

[2]Further details of the definitions and methods of our survey of budget obligations appear in the Appendix, and detailed breakdowns by individual agency appear in Abramson (1978). In one respect, however, our analytical quarry remained out of range. Although a great deal can be found out by classifying funding programs, each of these programs includes a number of individually funded projects, which may differ from one another in terms that bear on our principles of classification. We sought wherever possible to reflect this variety by apportioning a program among two or more categories, but refining these judgments by extending our survey to many thousands of individual projects would have swamped our resources. We note where our findings might be modified if they were rooted in data on individual projects.

[3]For a detailed discussion of demonstrations, see Cheryl D. Hayes, "Toward a Conceptualization of the Function of Demonstrations," hereafter cited as Hayes, "Demonstrations," *in* Glennan (1978).

TABLE 1   Funding Patterns: Social Knowledge Production and Application Activities (fiscal 1976 obligations, $ millions)

Activity	$	%
Knowledge production		
Research	655	36
Demonstrations for policy formulation	204	11
Program evaluation	62	3
General purpose statistics	294	16
Total	1,215	67
Knowledge application		
Demonstrations for policy implementation	183	10
Development of materials	121	7
Dissemination	294	16
Total	598	33
TOTAL	1,813	100

Numbers may not total due to rounding.

NOTE: Caution should be used when making comparisons between the data above and the data on "research and development" collected by the National Science Foundation and the Office of Management and Budget. As noted in Chapter 1, several of the above categories fall outside the definition of R&D used by the federal government. Thus, the $1.8 billion total should not be interpreted as being part of total federal obligations for research and development. A fuller discussion of these data and definitions appears in the Appendix.

for the development of materials, our categories of knowledge application have traditionally been excluded from figures on R&D. This is true of the largest of our categories, the activities we group under "dissemination." This figure is almost certainly on the low side, since it includes only separately identifiable projects for dissemination. Nonetheless, this and the other figures in these categories indicate the general magnitude of recent explicit federal investment in the application of knowledge to social problems.

FUNDING PATTERNS BY POLICY AREA

In addition to providing estimates of the amounts spent for social knowledge production and application, our survey sought to provide a basis for analyzing the allocation of funding by subject. Working with a classification of policy areas similar to those proposed by the General Accounting Office and the House Budget Committee, we identified twelve areas, grouped in four broad categories: human resources, community resources, natural resources, and science and technology. The human resources category includes health, education, employment and training, and social services and income security. The community services category includes economic growth, transportation, housing and community development, law enforcement and justice, and international affairs. The natural resources category includes natural resources and the environment and energy development and conservation. Finally, the science and technology category includes a set of programs designed to strengthen the nation's science and technology base.

Table 2 presents the distribution of support for social knowledge production and application among the twelve policy areas. Human resources claim about 60 percent of the total, with community resources, including economic growth, accounting for another 28 percent. The table discloses interesting variations in funding for knowledge production and for knowledge application among policy areas. For example:

• In education, there is a high proportion of funding for knowledge application (60 percent) as opposed to knowledge production. This is because most of this work is supported by the practitioner-dominated Office of Education; emphasis has been placed on policy implementation demonstrations and the development of materials rather than on research.

• In health, in contrast, the proportions are almost exactly the opposite. Much of this spending for knowledge production can be traced to the National Institutes of Health, which have placed much greater emphasis on basic research and the creation of new knowledge than on the application of existing knowledge. This emphasis has influenced the activities of many agencies that are concerned with social problems related to health.

• In social services and income security, there is little funding for knowledge application, largely because policy makers who use such research are federal officials, and so dissemination can be informal.

Table 3 shows how the relative allocation of social knowledge production and application obligations among the policy areas compares with the relative allocation of the total federal budget authority (including knowledge production and application, operating programs, administrative expenses, etc.) among comparable policy areas.

Two observations can be made from these figures. The first is that the federal investment in social knowledge production and application

TABLE 2   Funding Patterns: Social Knowledge Production and Application by Policy Area (fiscal 1976 obligations, $ millions)

Policy Area	Knowledge Production		Knowledge Application		Total	
	$	%	$	%	$	%
Human resources						
Health	265	61	171	39	436 (24)[a]	100
Education	156	40	237	60	394 (22)	100
Employment and training	118	85	21	15	139 (8)	100
Social services and income security	92	82	21	18	112 (6)	100
Total	631		450		1,081 (60)	
Community resources						
Economic growth	178	86	29	14	206 (11)	100
Transportation	84	74	29	26	114 (6)	100
Housing and community development	62	58	45	42	106 (6)	100
Law enforcement and justice	47	72	18	28	65 (4)	100
International affairs	17	73	6	27	23 (1)	100
Total	388		127		514 (28)	
Natural resources						
Natural resources and environment	111	97	4	3	114 (6)	100
Energy development and conservation	28	95	2	5	30 (2)	100
Total	139		6		144 (8)	
Science and technology base	58	78	16	22	74 (4)	100
TOTAL	1,215		598		1,813 (100)	

Numbers may not total due to rounding.
[a]Numbers in parentheses are column percentages.

TABLE 3   Comparison of Funding Patterns for Social Knowledge Production and Application with Total Federal Civilian Budget by Policy Area (fiscal 1976 obligations, $ millions)

Policy Area	Funding for Knowledge Production and Application		Total Civilian Budget[a]		Funding for Knowledge Production and Application (Col. 1)/ Total Civilian Budget (Col. 3)
	$	%	$	%	
Human resources					
Health	436	24	32,339	11	0.013
Education	394	22	7,889	3	0.050
Employment and training	139	8	7,910	3	0.018
Social services and income security	112	6	144,281	48	0.001
Total	1,081	60	192,419	64	0.006
Community resources					
Economic growth	(206)[b]	(11)[b]	No comparable OMB function		
Transportation	114	6	9,906	3	0.012
Housing and community development[c]	106	6	14,332	5	0.007
Law enforcement and justice	65	4	3,264	1	0.020
International affairs	23	1	6,450	2	0.004
Total	308	17	33,952	11	0.009
Natural resources					
Natural resources and environment	114	6	15,667	5	0.007
Energy development and conservation	30	2	3,522	1	0.009
Total	144	8	19,189	6	0.008
Science and technology base	74	4	1,145	*	0.065
Other civilian functions[d]			56,132	19	
TOTAL	1,813	100	302,837[e]	100	0.006

Numbers may not total due to rounding.
[a]Source: *The Budget of the United States Government,* Fiscal 1977, Part 8, Tables 2 and 14.
[b]Excluded from subtotal.
[c]Includes OMB function of revenue sharing in addition to community and regional development.
[d]Includes agriculture, commerce, veterans' benefits, general government, interest, allowances, and undistributed offsetting receipts.
[e]National defense and space research and technology are excluded from budget total.
*Less than 0.5 percent.

represents a small though varied fraction of total program costs. For all policy areas, this fraction averages only six-tenths of one percent (0.006). In the special case of science and technology, where R&D outlays (mainly nonsocial) account for most of the total, the fraction invested in social knowledge production and application is still only seven percent. Of the substantive policy areas, only in education, where program costs are primarily met from nonfederal sources, is the investment in social knowledge production and application more than two percent of total program costs.

The second observation is that there is a rough equivalence between the fraction that a policy category claims of the whole federal budget, on the one hand, and of the federal investment in social knowledge production and application, on the other. These two fractions tend to vary together in the totals for the four policy categories of human resources, community resources, natural resources, and science and technology. At this level of aggregation, support for social knowledge production and application does appear to "follow the budget." But the variation at the level of policy area is considerable and shows, for example, how relatively slight is the investment in the creation and use of knowledge on social services and income security.

FUNDING PATTERNS BY AGENCY

The most revealing findings to emerge from our survey of spending for social knowledge production and application have to do with the organizational location of the programs of support. Table 4 presents data on levels of fiscal 1976 federal support for knowledge production and application at the level of the department or independent agency. These data show how much of the spending is accounted for by a few departments and agencies. Of the 44 organizational entities summarized in the table, the Department of Health, Education, and Welfare is the largest supporter of social knowledge production and application, accounting for nearly 40 percent of the total—almost $730 million. Four other departments spent over $100 million on social knowledge production and application in fiscal 1976, and a total of 23 agencies spent more than $5 million.

There is further evidence on this point in Table 5, which lists the 20 agencies with the largest budgets for social knowledge production and application; they account for 71.6 percent of the $1.8 billion total. Significantly, these agencies represent a wide spectrum of types of mission and activity. The largest agency, the Office of Education (OE), comprises primarily operating programs. Although research is not a major priority, OE has seen education innovation as a program goal for at least the past 15 years and obligates a substantial portion of its funds to demonstration activities. Three of the 20 agencies—the National Science Foundation, the National Institutes of Health, and the National Institute of Education—specialize primarily in research; two—the Bureau of the Census and the Bureau of Labor Statistics—are statistical agencies that also have the support of knowledge production and application activities as a primary mission.[4] As might be expected, given HEW's share of total social knowledge production and application spending, 9 of the 20 are HEW agencies.

But the evidence on organizational location should not be misread: 180 distinct federal agencies are involved in funding social knowledge production and application activities, and many of the agencies on the top-20 list are aggregates of a number of smaller and fairly autonomous funding programs. Indeed, the decentralization of the funding effort is striking.

Decentralization has been the natural consequence of the way authorization has been given for programs of support of social research and development. The prevailing approach is clearly reflected in authorizing legislation. A recent compilation of R&D statutes by the Congressional Research Service for the House Committee on Science and Technology found that ". . . most Federal R&D laws appear to relate to 'mission oriented' research and development and to be administered by agencies directly involved with specific missions and responsibilities" (U.S. Congress, House 1976b, p. 3). The major exceptions are the statutes dealing with the National Science Foundation and the Smithsonian Institution, agencies whose legislation provides a clear mandate to broad areas of basic research.

This evidence led David ("Two Transformations," *in* Stokes 1978), in analyzing the emerging federal role in social research and development, to conclude that the commitment of federal funds has largely been shaped by policy and program legislation that only incidentally contained provisions authorizing or directing the conduct of mission-related R&D. In other words, the legal and political basis for R&D activities within an agency has followed, rather than preceded, the policy and program commitments that specify the agency's purpose and responsibilities—its mission. This pattern accounts for the location of most R&D programs within the operating federal departments rather

[4]For more information on the role of the primary and secondary statistical agencies of the federal government, see President's Commission on Federal Statistics (1971).

TABLE 4 Funding Patterns: Social Knowledge Production and Application Activities by Department or Agency (fiscal 1976 obligations, $ millions)

Department or Agency	Knowledge Production Activities					Knowledge Application Activities				TOTAL
	Re-search	Policy Formula-tion Dem-onstrations	Program Evalu-ation	General Purpose Statistics	Total	Policy Implemen-tation Dem-onstrations	Develop-ment of Materials	Dissem-ination	Total	
Department of Agriculture	62	*	3	41	106	—	1	176	177	282
Department of Commerce	22	4	2	77	106	1	*	7	8	114
Department of Defense	40	2	*	2	45	—	13	1	14	58
Department of Health, Educa-tion, and Welfare[a]										
Health Related[b]	139	34	9	31	212	37	6	33	76	287
Education[c]	46	81	17	4	149	79	54	23	156	305
Income Security[d]	20	21	2	—	43	2	—	1	3	46
Human Development[e]	38	19	10	2	70	12	2	7	21	91
Total—Department of Health, Education, and Welfare	243	155	38	37	474	130	62	64	256	729
Department of Housing and Urban Development	10	19	4	11	44	7	3	5	14	58
Department of the Interior	9	—	1	2	12	*	1	1	1	13
Department of Justice	28	*	5	13	47	12	—	6	18	65
Department of Labor	19	3	2	68	92	2	6	7	15	107
Department of State	14	1	2	—	17	1	*	6	7	24
Department of Transportation	43	9	1	21	74	10	8	10	27	101
Department of the Treasury	11	—	—	15	25	—	—	—	—	25
Appalachian Regional Commission	1	4	1	—	5	8	—	—	8	13

Civil Service Commission	2	—	*	*	3	2	1	—	3	6
Commission on Civil Rights	5	—	—	—	5	—	—	2	2	7
Community Services Administration	2	1	—	—	3	5	—	—	5	8
Energy Research and Development Administration	12	—	—	—	12	—	—	—	—	12
Environmental Protection Agency	12	—	1	—	13	—	—	—	—	13
Executive Office of the President[f]	4	—	*	*	4	—	—	1	1	6
Federal Reserve System	6	—	—	3	9	—	—	—	—	9
National Foundation on the Arts and the Humanities	1	—	*	*	1	—	14	3	17	18
National Science Foundation	76	2	1	1	80	3	13	*	17	97
Smithsonian Institution	8	—	*	*	8	—	*	1	1	10
Veterans Administration	2	2	1	—	5	2	—	2	2	7
Independent agencies[g]	15	—	*	*	15	1	—	1	1	16
Other agencies[h]	8	1	2	1	12	1	—	3	4	15
TOTAL	655	204	62	294	1,215	183	121	293	598	1,813

Numbers may not total due to rounding.

[a] The activities of the Assistant Secretary for Planning and Evaluation have been included throughout the four policy areas.

[b] Alcohol, Drug Abuse, and Mental Health Administration; Center for Disease Control; Food and Drug Administration; Health Resources Administration; Health Services Administration; National Institutes of Health; and Assistant Secretary for Health.

[c] National Institute of Education; Office of Education; Assistant Secretary for Education.

[d] Social and Rehabilitation Service; Social Security Administration.

[e] Office of Human Development.

[f] Council of Economic Advisors; Council on Environmental Quality; Office of Telecommunications; Council on Wage and Price Stability.

[g] Civil Aeronautics Board; Consumer Product Safety Commission; Federal Communications Commission; Federal Home Loan Bank Board; Federal Power Commission; International Trade Commission; Interstate Commerce Commission; Nuclear Regulatory Commission; Securities and Exchange Commission; Federal Trade Commission.

[h] ACTION; Federal Mediation and Conciliation Service; General Services Administration; Small Business Administration; United States Information Agency; Arms Control and Disarmament Agency; National Center for Productivity and Quality of Working Life; Advisory Commission on Intergovernmental Relations; Federal Energy Administration; Equal Employment Opportunity Commission; Tennessee Valley Authority.

*Less than $0.5 million.

TABLE 5 Twenty Agencies with Largest Budgets for Social Knowledge Production and Application (fiscal 1976 obligations, $ millions)

Agency	Department	Knowledge Production	Knowledge Application	Total
1. Office of Education	HEW	89	124	213
2. Extension Service	USDA	2	166	168
3. National Science Foundation		80	17	97
4. Alcohol, Drug Abuse, and Mental Health Administration	HEW	78	7	85
5. Office of Human Development	HEW	55	21	76
6. National Institute of Education	HEW	46	28	74
7. Health Resources Administration	HEW	55	13	68
8. Bureau of the Census	Commerce	65	1	67
9. National Institutes of Health	HEW	42	22	64
10. Bureau of Labor Statistics	Labor	56	–	56
11. Policy Development and Research	HUD	50	5	55
12. Law Enforcement Assistance Administration	Justice	41	18	58
13. Health Services Administration	HEW	21	31	52
14. Assistant Secretary for Planning and Evaluation	HEW	34	–	34
15. Statistical Reporting Service	USDA	31	–	31
16. Economic Research Service	USDA	25	6	31
17. National Highway Traffic Safety Administration	DOT	17	10	27
18. Social Security Administration	HEW	25	1	26
19. Cooperative State Research Service	USDA	25	–	25
20. Office of the Secretary	DOT	20	4	24
TOTAL		857	473	1,330

Numbers may not total due to rounding.

than in independent R&D agencies. It also accounts for the decentralization of R&D programs to several mission agencies within major departments.

The mission-related character of much of the federal support of the production and application of knowledge of social problems can be summarized by classifying the organizations in which the programs are located. For this purpose, we developed a fourfold categorization of supporting agencies:

Associated with operating programs. Offices that have programmatic responsibility to administer federal programs: for example, Food and Nutrition Service (Agriculture); Economic Development Administration (Commerce); Office of Education (HEW); National Park Service (Interior); and the Federal Highway Administration (Transportation).

Associated with policy-making offices. Offices that do not directly administer programs and that frequently have oversight responsibility for a number of federal programs or have staff advisory responsibility for nonprogrammatic federal policies: for example, the Office of the Assistant Secretary for Planning and Evaluation (HEW); the Office of Planning, Budgeting, and Evaluation (Office of Education/HEW); Advisory Commission on Intergovernmental Relations; U.S. Commission on Civil Rights; and the Council of Economic Advisers.

Associated with agencies whose primary mission is R&D funding. For example: the National Institute of Education (HEW); the Agricultural Research Service (Agriculture); the National Center for Health Services Research (HEW); and the National Science Foundation.

Associated with agencies whose primary mission is the collection or analysis of statistics. For example: Statistical Reporting Service (Agriculture); Bureau of the Census (Commerce); National Center for Education Statistics (HEW); and the National Criminal Justice Information and Statistical Service (Law Enforcement Assistance Administration/Justice).

Table 6 presents data on the allocation of federal support for knowledge production and application in fiscal 1976 by this classification. Although some agencies were difficult to categorize, the data show the extent to which program operations influence social knowledge production and application. More than 50 percent of total social knowledge production and application obligations—more than 75 percent of

TABLE 6 Funding Patterns: Type of Supporting Agency by Social Knowledge Production and Application Activities (fiscal 1976 obligations, $ millions)

| | Type of Supporting Agency | | | | | | | | | |
| | Operating Programs | | Policy-Making Offices | | R&D Funding Agencies | | Statistical Agencies | | Total | |
Activity	$	%	$	%	$	%	$	%	$	%
Knowledge production										
Research	258 (28)a	39	70 (40)	11	311 (63)	48	16 (8)	3	655 (36)	100
Policy formulation demonstrations	109 (12)	53	37 (21)	18	59 (12)	29	–	–	204 (11)	100
Program evaluation	28 (3)	46	25 (14)	40	9 (2)	14	* (*)	*	62 (3)	100
General purpose statistics	73 (8)	25	21 (12)	7	3 (1)	1	197 (91)	67	294 (16)	100
Total	468 (50)	39	152 (87)	13	382 (78)	31	213 (99)	18	1,215 (67)	100
Knowledge application										
Policy implementation demonstrations	166 (18)	91	7 (4)	4	10 (2)	6	–	–	183 (10)	100
Development of materials	72 (8)	59	3 (2)	2	46 (9)	38	–	–	121 (7)	100
Dissemination	224 (24)	76	12 (7)	4	55 (11)	19	3 (1)	1	294 (16)	100
Total	462 (50)	77	22 (13)	4	111 (23)	19	3 (1)	*	598 (33)	100
TOTAL	930 (100)	51	174 (100)	10	493 (100)	27	216 (100)	12	1,813 (100)	100

Numbers may not total due to rounding.   aNumbers in parentheses are column percentages.   *Less than $0.5 million or 0.5 percent.

the support for knowledge application activities—is associated with operating programs. In contrast, only 27 percent of total social knowledge production and application support is channeled through R&D agencies, although these are the agencies most usually associated with federal support of social knowledge production and application in the minds of investigators and the public. Furthermore, despite the increased emphasis on research to support policy making in recent years, less than 10 percent of federally supported social knowledge production and application is directly associated with offices primarily performing policy-making functions.[5]

Further findings emerge from the data in Table 6. R&D agencies support 47 percent of all research, while agencies associated with operating programs support another 40 percent. Approximately 70 percent of support for the production of social statistics is centered in a relatively small number of agencies and programs that specialize in statistical activities. The bulk of the relatively small amount of support for program evaluations, 86 percent, is administered by agencies associated with operating programs and policy-making offices.

A general conclusion that emerges from the data in Table 6 is the diversity of knowledge production and application activities supported by all except the statistical agencies. Every category of social knowledge production and application is carried out at a multimillion dollar level by agencies associated with operating programs, agencies associated with policy-making functions, and R&D agencies. For example, although more than half of policy-formulation demonstrations are associated with operating programs, significant support for such demonstrations comes from other types of agencies as well. Similarly, all types of agencies are involved in producing general purpose statistics.

FUNDING PATTERNS BY GOAL AND AUDIENCE

It would be easy to conclude from the prominence of operating program agencies among the supporters of social knowledge production and application that these activities are intended primarily to serve users in the federal government. But such an inference would miss a critical aspect of the intent of those activities, an aspect by no means obvious when we began our study. To describe the goal and audience

---

[5]We do not by this mean to exclude the possibility that some of the activities supported by mission agencies are directed to policy questions. Plainly they are, in some cases in response to the wishes of departmental policy offices.

of social knowledge production and application, we devised a fivefold classification of the objectives of the funding agencies:

- the improvement of federal programs;
- the improvement of federal policies;
- the creation and provision of knowledge and developed programs or materials for nonfederal audiences—knowledge for third parties;
- the general advancement of knowledge concerning individual and social behavior without specific concern for application; and
- the collection and analysis of statistics.

This categorization proved to be substantially more difficult and judgmental than the categorization according to organizational location and function. For example, the National Institute of Mental Health (NIMH) supports considerable basic disciplinary research as well as research centered on a variety of social and mental health problems. It also supports a significant amount of research that is intended to be useful to practitioners in community mental health centers, social service agencies, and third parties generally. Although the political rhetoric surrounding the program emphasizes the latter activity, we concluded the predominant function of NIMH to be the advancement of knowledge and classified the agency accordingly.[6]

As shown in Table 7, important findings emerge from the data on total spending by major goal and audience. First, third-party interests dominate federal interests: more than 50 percent of all federal support is by agencies whose primary function is the production and application of knowledge for nonfederal audiences. The combined federal social knowledge production and application obligations by agencies whose primary goal is the improvement of federal programs and the improvement of federal policies are less than 25 percent of the total. Thus, spending on behalf of third-party (nonfederal) audiences is apparently greater than spending for first-party (federal) audiences by a ratio of more than two to one.

Second, only about 10 percent of all federal spending for social knowledge production and application is for the advancement of knowledge without specific concern for application. The bulk of support for the production and application of knowledge related to social problems, more than 75 percent, is administered by agencies whose primary goal is the improvement or formulation of programs and policies.

[6]Clearly, we would have gained added information on goals and audience by carrying the analysis to the level of individual projects if this had been feasible.

TABLE 7 Funding Patterns: Goal or Audience by Social Knowledge Production and Application Activities (fiscal 1976 obligations, $ millions)

| | Goal or Audience | | | | | | | | | | | |
| | Improvement of Federal Programs | | Improvement of Federal Policy | | Knowledge for Third Parties | | Advancement of Knowledge | | Statistical Collection | | Total | |
Activity	$	%	$	%	$	%	$	%	$	%	$	%
Knowledge production	206	17	170	14	443	37	167	14	230	19	1,215	100
	(82)[a]		(90)		(47)		(86)		(99)		(67)	
Knowledge application	44	7	18	3	506	85	27	5	3	*	598	100
	(18)		(10)		(53)		(14)		(1)		(33)	
TOTAL	250	14	188	10	948	52	194	11	232	3	1,813	100
	(100)		(100)		(100)		(100)		(100)		(100)	

Number may not total due to rounding.
[a]Numbers in parentheses are column percentages.
*Less than 0.5 percent.

31

Table 8 presents a cross-classification of total social knowledge production and application obligations by organizational location and function and by major goal and audience. It is significant to note that of the total federal support associated with operating programs and policy-making offices, more than 72 percent was intended for use by third-party audiences; only 26 percent was intended for the use of federal officials in the improvement of federal programs. Thus, nonfederal audiences have a major stake in the policies and practices governing federal support for knowledge production and application.

A much smaller portion of the funds for social knowledge production and application is spent by agencies (or their subdivisions) that have as a primary mission the improvement of federal programs or policies. More than half of the total for social knowledge production and application is spent by offices that have as a primary audience nonfederal decision makers, with most of the remainder spent by offices that have as a primary goal the advancement of knowledge without specific concern for application.

CONCLUSIONS

Several conclusions about the system of federal support for social knowledge production and application emerge from the patterns of funding examined in this chapter.

First, the types of activity are far more varied than the term "social R&D" suggests. They include a wide range of activities concerned with the production and use of knowledge of social problems. Indeed, research, as it would generally be understood by the research community, claimed no more than 36 percent of the total obligations of $1.8 billion in fiscal 1976. More than one-third of these obligations was for applications of knowledge of social problems.

Second, the policy areas to which this spending is directed also cover a broad range. Approximately 60 percent of the total is concerned with human resources, and community resources accounts for 28 percent. There is wide variation among policy areas in the division of support between knowledge-producing and knowledge-applying activities. In every policy area, the federal government invests part of its total spending for the production and use of social knowledge, but this fraction is an exceedingly small part of total program costs in every area and averages only six-tenths of one percent for all policy areas.

Third, the organizational location of funding programs shows a strong pattern of decentralization. Because the federal investment has

TABLE 8 Funding Patterns: Organizational Location by Goal or Audience (fiscal 1976 obligations, $ millions)

| | Organizational Location | | | | | | | | | |
| | Associated with Operating Programs | | Associated with Policy-Making Offices | | Associated with R&D Funding Agencies | | Associated with Statistical Agencies | | Total | |
Goal or Audience	$	%	$	%	$	%	$	%	$	%
Improvement of federal programs	243 (26)[a]	97	–	–	7 (1)	3	–	–	250 (14)	100
Improvement of federal policies	13 (1)	7	144 (82)	77	31 (6)	17	–	–	188 (10)	100
Knowledge for third parties	670 (72)	71	18 (10)	2	260 (53)	27	–	–	948 (52)	100
Advancement of knowledge	–	–	–	–	194 (39)	100	–	–	194 (11)	100
Statistical collection	4 (*)	2	13 (7)	5	–	–	216 (100)	93	232 (13)	100
TOTAL	930 (100)	51	174 (100)	10	493 (100)	27	216 (100)	12	1,183 (100)	100

Numbers may not total due to rounding.
[a]Numbers in parentheses are column percentages.
*Less than 0.5 percent.

33

been a corollary of the creation and assignment of social programs to mission agencies, more than half of federal support of social knowledge production and application is associated with mission agencies, with much smaller amounts associated with departmental policy offices, independent R&D agencies, and specialized statistical agencies. This pattern means that the departments and agencies with the heaviest responsibilities for social programs also tend to have the largest aggregate budgets for social knowledge production and application. Indeed, the combined obligations within the Department of Health, Education, and Welfare account for roughly 40 percent of the total for the entire executive branch. Of the 180 agencies that support social knowledge production and application, the 20 with the largest budgets account for more than 70 percent of the total expenditures.

Fourth, the audiences of social knowledge production and application activities lie to a remarkable degree outside the federal government. Spending on behalf of third-party users exceeds spending for federal users by a ratio of more than two to one. This ratio is even higher if one considers only the support for social knowledge production and application that is associated with the mission agencies. Only 10 percent of the total is spent by agencies primarily concerned with the advancement of knowledge.

3 The Management of Federal Support for Social Knowledge Production and Application

The patterns of funding explored in Chapter 2 show the outlines of the system of federal support for social knowledge production and application, but a sense of how the system operates can be gained only by probing beneath the surface of those budget data. This chapter summarizes the findings and conclusions on organization and management we derived from two groups of studies. The first is a set of analyses of managerial problems—particularly those of staffing, the choice of instruments of support, and the role of demonstrations—that are common to all agencies supporting social knowledge production and application (Glennan 1978). The second is a set of case studies of the management of R&D programs in the policy areas of health, income security, the enhancement of the living environment, and development in early childhood (Lynn 1978b).

Many of the detailed findings of these studies show more clearly the aspects of the system already apparent in the funding data. This is particularly true of its decentralized character, which follows the categorical nature of the process of congressional authorization and appropriations, a process that has by the mid-1970s created nearly 1,100 identifiable domestic programs. The compartmentalized organization and management typical of categorical programs is also typical of the research and development activities associated with these programs. For example, research on early childhood is supported by 16 separate agencies within HEW (7 within the Office of Education alone)

35

and by agencies within 3 other departments as well,[1] and 50 departments and agencies support health-related social knowledge production and application.[2]

The detailed studies of organization and management also allowed us to examine characteristics of the system that cannot be discerned in funding patterns alone. These findings are summarized under three general headings: setting research agendas, disseminating and applying results, and managing the system.

SETTING RESEARCH AGENDAS

We found that the general content and emphasis of research agendas are shaped largely by factors external to the agencies supporting social knowledge production and application. A variety of interests and forces influence the selection of issues and problems on which these agencies support research: special interest constituencies; congressional concerns, often expressed in terms of statutory mandates to do particular kinds of studies; the priorities of policy-making officials in federal agencies; and the interests of social knowledge production and application performers. For example, research administrators come to know which types or topics of research are popular with the Office of Management and Budget (OMB), congressional committees, or advocacy groups, and which will attract criticism and opposition. As one observer noted: "A vote to support a $30 million effort to cure diabetes goes down a lot better with constituents than a vote to spend $300,000 to investigate co-insurance schemes for Medicare." Our special study of demonstration projects showed how influential political factors are in setting the agenda of this particular form of social knowledge production and application (see Hayes, "Demonstrations," *in* Glennan 1978).

These observations are hardly surprising. Because social knowledge production and application must be legitimized through the political process, the participants in this process will leave their mark on research agendas. More significant is the finding that forces bearing on research agendas are responded to largely in ad hoc, reactive fashion.

[1]See Christine L. Davis and Cheryl D. Hayes, "Early Childhood: The Content and Management of Social Research and Development in Selected Federal Agencies," hereafter cited as Davis and Hayes, "Early Childhood," *in* Lynn (1978b).
[2]See John M. Seidl and Christine L. Davis, "The Management of Social Research and Development in Federal Health Agencies," hereafter cited as Seidl and Davis, "Health," *in* Lynn (1978b).

We seldom found agency management activities that could be described as "planning," i.e., the systematic derivation of research agendas from an analysis of the issues or problems with which the agency should be concerned, their "researchability," and the potential benefits to those with a stake in research results. Although many federal research administrators speak in terms of goals and plans, detailed examination shows that these rationales are usually after the fact; decisions on the initiation of research are largely ad hoc and piecemeal.[3]

Research administrators also seldom involve the potential users of research findings in the process of setting research agendas. Although users represent an important constituent group and have influence in a variety of ways, their ideas and priorities are not systematically brought into the research planning process. Even in agencies where research programs are directly tied to operating service programs, there is frequently a lack of communication and cooperation between research administrators and program management staff. Research objectives and the needs of operating programs are not often synchronized; planning efforts and operational policies are poorly coordinated. Research administrators who retain control over the research purse strings are frequently unresponsive to the ideas and priorities of the potential users of their research (see Davis and Hayes, "Early Childhood," *in* Lynn 1978b).

The prominent exceptions to this general finding are in such policy areas as health and transportation, which have a strong core of science and technology. In these areas, researchers and users of research have similar training and professional norms and mutually support one another (see Hayes, "Demonstrations," *in* Glennan 1978). Other notable exceptions are situations in which research administrators have developed close ties with powerful congressional sponsors, trade associations, advocacy groups, or agency policy makers in order to ensure adequate and continuous support. Agribusiness interest groups, for example, are particularly influential in shaping Department of Agriculture research programs; they also constitute a well-informed consumer constituency.[4]

There have been several attempts to involve users in research

---

[3]For a detailed account of research planning on early childhood, see Davis and Hayes, "Early Childhood," *in* Lynn (1978b). The planning of health services research is discussed in Seidl and Davis, "Health," *in* Lynn (1978b).

[4]See John M. Seidl, "The Management of Social Research and Development in the Federal Government's Living Environment Agencies," hereafter cited as Seidl, "Living Environment," *in* Lynn (1978b).

planning through conferences or periodic panel meetings. For example, the Maternal and Child Health Service, within the Bureau of Community Health Services in HEW, appoints "lay person-consumers" to their panels evaluating grant applications (see Davis and Hayes, "Early Childhood," in Lynn 1978b). On the whole, however, these efforts fail to influence research agendas because they do not lead to sustained communication between research administrators and user representatives; mutual understanding rarely develops.

Coordination and Gaps in Research

Despite the fragmentation of responsibility for research in particular policy areas, we found little evidence of duplication of effort. Funding agencies seek assiduously to differentiate their knowledge production and application activities from those of other agencies—lest the budget axe fall. Rumored instances of overlap usually turn out to be cases in which researchers from different professions or disciplines are studying quite different questions under the same policy heading. When actual or potential overlap occurs—occasionally central grant administration offices find they can assign a grant application to two or more different offices—some basis for differentiating and compartmentalizing the related activities is usually found.

We did find that numerous aspects of large policy or problem areas are not being adequately pursued, either because they are not perceived as being specifically within the mission of any one funding agency or because they are vaguely within the domains of more than one agency. The problem of meeting the nutritional needs of children is an example: the Office of Child Development (in HEW), the Maternal and Child Health Service (within the Bureau of Community Health Services in HEW), the Social and Rehabilitation Service (in HEW), and the Department of Agriculture all have interests and potential responsibility in this area. Rather than infringe on the turf of any of the others, none has taken the lead. Consequently, there is limited research on certain aspects of the nutritional needs of children.

We also found that little coordination occurs among agencies. The substantial efforts needed to transcend agency interests and initiate research programs addressed to broad social problems are seldom undertaken (see Davis and Hayes, "Early Childhood," in Lynn 1978b). Perhaps the main disincentive to such efforts is the fact that there are no visible constituencies in Congress or the executive branch for the results of research that cuts across the interests of several agencies—cross-cutting research. Furthermore, "oversight" institutions—the domestic policy staff in the White House, OMB, the central planning and budgeting offices of federal agencies, congressional appropriations committees, and the General Accounting Office—currently devote scant attention to overcoming the forces that discourage unified and coordinated action and dissipate the benefits that could be realized from social knowledge production and application programs. Our study of the management of social R&D on the living environment has documented the ineffectiveness of oversight institutions in promoting cross-cutting research (see Seidl, "Living Environment," *in* Lynn 1978b).

In general, there is a lack of both interest in and methods for allocating resources among competing social policy areas. Since social problems usually encompass the missions and interests of several federal agencies, planning would require coordinating their knowledge production and application activities. We did find several instances of joint funding of research programs, but these were usually well-defined studies that were too expensive to be funded by a single agency. Overall, we did not find any sustained cooperative planning effort to establish program goals for social knowledge production and application activities of interest to two or more agencies, nor a systematic sharing and synthesis of the findings generated by different but related agencies, nor evaluation of the research of related programs for its applicability to the programs of different organizational entities.

An instructive exception is provided by the agencies, such as the Bureau of the Census, that have responsibility for statistical programs. A professional commitment to render a service and the need to share some of the costs of data collection have led in many cases to collaborative planning by the producing agencies and the governmental and nongovernmental consumers of their output.

Finally, we found that little attention is given to forecasting social problems in order to direct current social knowledge production and application investments for greatest long-run value.

The Role of Incentives

Those in the executive and legislative branches who might encourage better research planning share the responsibility for the defects of agenda setting: we found few tangible incentives for systematic and imaginative planning of social knowledge production and application. The research administrator who ensures that new projects and renewals occur on schedule, that appropriated funds are spent, and that constituencies are satisfied will survive nicely without a plan. Establishing a systematic research agenda takes time and qualified staff for effective outreach to the research and user communities, and these resources are invariably in short supply. Without incentives, research administrators are not apt to divert scarce time and talent to activities that can seem to be abstract exercises with little impact on the growth or survival of their agencies.

Indeed, many of the management controls on agencies supporting the production and use of knowledge—such as OMB clearance of research questionnaires and field interviews, regulations on agency staffing and promotions, and constraints on the use of grants and contracts—frequently exacerbate the weaknesses of research adminis- tration. The resort to management controls is a natural tendency of those who must oversee a decentralized system with widely recurring problems, but these controls do not offer research administrators positive incentives for creative planning of research agendas.

DISSEMINATING AND APPLYING RESULTS

We found that among the agencies supporting social knowledge pro- duction and application, conscious emphasis on disseminating research results ranges from heavy to nonexistent.[5] With few exceptions—of which the most notable were in the Department of Agriculture and in HEW (particularly the Social Security Administration, the National Institute of Education, and parts of the National Institute of Mental Health)—we found little developed policy concerning dissemination or application (see Seidl and Davis, "Health," in Lynn 1978b).

Reasons for Neglect

One reason for the lack of policy is that there often is little to disseminate and little need for dissemination efforts. Research adminis- trators are understandably chary of pressing research results on poten- tial users when they have doubts themselves about either the quality of the research or the relevance of the results.

Beyond this, two reasons appear to account for the lack of emphasis on dissemination. First, there is little agreement inside or outside the government concerning the appropriate federal role in disseminating research results. In general, dissemination tends to be no one's respon-

[5]See Daniel M. Katz, "Survey Methodology: Its Development, Utilization, and Poten- tial," hereafter cited as Katz, "Survey Methodology," in Stokes (1978), and Davis and Hayes, "Early Childhood," in Lynn (1978b).

sibility: it is not an important aspect of the responsibilities of research administrators or performers. Bureaucratic incentives to disseminate findings are weak and often conflicting. Research findings may be politically and scientifically controversial, and research managers may be reluctant to be put into the defensive role that publishing such results will tend to thrust on them. Moreover, management attention is usually focused on bread-and-butter matters, such as budgets, new projects, and renewals. The performance of research administrators is rarely judged on whether the findings of completed research are being disseminated.

Second, administrators with academic orientations, or those whose research activities are academically oriented, believe they have an automatic dissemination mechanism: the academic publications process. This channel has the advantage of providing automatic quality control since academic journals presumably publish only the results of well-done, worthwhile research endeavors. But administrators who for some reason cannot rely on this mechanism typically have no alternative system for making research results accessible to interested audiences.

Several agencies have taken steps to improve dissemination. One is the practice of depositing approved research reports in the National Technical Information Service (NTIS), a part of the Department of Commerce, or other research abstract or report library. Although these computerized retrieval systems can be useful, they present a number of difficulties. Their coding procedures often make it difficult to locate particular research reports. Moreover, because these systems do not synthesize or analyze for quality or relevance, they may turn out reams of undigested research findings that overwhelm potential users. As a consequence, research results that are filed with NTIS or other similar retrieval systems are seldom useful to federal or third-party policy makers, who do not have the time to read and evaluate masses of research reports. (They may, however, be quite useful to other researchers.)

Other efforts by federal agencies to improve dissemination include requiring researchers to prepare executive summaries of their work and comply with other guidelines for final reports; creating dissemination offices; requiring dissemination plans from contractors and grantees; and promoting new media for reporting research results—such as *Evaluation* magazine supported by the National Institute of Mental Health (NIMH) and the Technical Analysis Papers series created by the Office of the Assistant Secretary for Planning and Evaluation in HEW. However, such efforts have frequently been thwarted by agency or

OMB hostility to expenditures for the publication of "self-serving" agency reports, to the subsidized distribution of materials, or to publication of politically sensitive findings.

Sense of Audience

In general, we found little evidence that research administrators have a clear sense of the appropriate audience for the research they support, even when they have definite expectations that findings will be published. Exceptions include instances when constituency pressures, communicated through Congress, take the form of specific mandates to "study and report" or when research needs are highly focused and insistent. Other exceptions occur when research has been under way for some time and earlier results have been disseminated and used, or when research is within the mainstream of a discipline or profession. As examples of the last, social R&D efforts supported by agencies of the Department of Agriculture and the Department of Transportation have well-developed audience networks. Researchers and users are frequently members of the same profession and view problems from similar perspectives; they share a common language and frame of reference, and they subscribe to the same professional journals and are on the same mailing lists (see Seidl, "Living Environment," *in* Lynn 1978b, and Hayes, "Demonstrations," *in* Glennan 1978).

When polled informally in our data survey, research managers frequently indicated that "everyone" was the audience. When pressed, many indicated that good results will generate their own audience or expressed reluctance to accept what they regard as an unduly restricted view of who will be interested in the work. The management studies confirm the existence of gaps between the researcher and the policy maker or other potential user. Researchers seldom begin by asking: What questions are potential users interested in? What are their intellectual and political perspectives? How are they likely to view research results? How should that affect what I do? Neither their training nor the norms of their profession prepare them to raise and answer such questions.[6]

As a result, a specific sense of audience seldom develops, even for research that is unquestionably considered applied research. This sense is particularly important in knowledge production or application activities that are tied to operating programs or directed to policy:

[6]For a discussion of the gap between policy makers and researchers in the Environmental Protection Agency and the Department of Housing and Urban Development, see Seidl, "Living Environment," *in* Lynn (1978b).

research that lacks a clearly specified audience frequently fails to be relevant to the needs of any audience. (A sense of audience is less crucial for knowledge production and application efforts that explore broad problem areas or seek fundamental advances in the knowledge and methods of the social sciences.)

Our study of demonstrations underscores the importance of a sense of audience in applied R&D activities. By our definitions, policy-formulation demonstrations test in an operational setting the political and administrative effectiveness of a particular mode of intervention on some social problem; they are meant to show federal policy makers whether and how a program should be implemented. Policy-implementation demonstrations are used to promote the adoption or adaptation of a particular program by federal policy makers, state or local policy makers, or practitioners. Demonstrations can be particularly effective in communicating with potential users because they are far more real and credible than written research reports; they can show not only that a program works effectively but how it works. Both policy-formulation and policy-implementation demonstrations are clearly applied endeavors, yet we found that those who manage demonstration projects are rarely alert to the needs of the wider audience they are meant to influence (see Hayes, "Demonstrations," *in* Glennan 1978).

Excessive Project Orientation

Little effort is devoted to synthesizing research knowledge or seeing the results of particular research projects as net additions to an existing body of knowledge. Aside from reviews of the literature, few efforts are made to determine how much is known about a given problem or issue from a comprehensive and interdisciplinary perspective. Project findings are disseminated with little attempt to place them in a substantive or intellectual context.[7]

The incentives that produce fragmentation and ad hoc, reactive decisions on research priorities clearly operate here as well. Incentives for a more effective synthesis of existing knowledge are rarely supplied by oversight institutions or the governmental users of research results.

[7]For a notable recent exception, see George et al. (1975), prepared for the Commission on the Organization of the Government for the Conduct of Foreign Policy. "By necessity," the authors note, "the present study has had to formulate an eclectic framework of its own within which to discuss and evaluate the many different kinds of findings and theories that are relevant to one or another aspect of the overall problem of improving the use of information in foreign policy decision making" (p. 7).

Those who must make short-term, incremental decisions on policies and programs do not look for fundamental insights on social functioning and human behavior. A policy process concerned with negotiating incremental changes to statutory authorities, budgets, and regulations generates no more than a weak demand for broad syntheses of knowledge.

Understanding the Process of Change

Research administrators rarely have a good understanding of the ways in which change occurs and innovations are adopted. In this they are in good company. Systematic studies of change, in particular of planned change, are of relatively recent origin and this type of research has for the most part focused on practitioners rather than policy makers. For example, "decision determinants analysis," pioneered by the Mental Health Services Utilization Branch of NIMH, assists mental health centers to assess their readiness to adopt changes in approach or practice.[8] Moreover, most studies of the process of change and the diffusion of innovation have been concerned with technological advances rather than with social developments.[9] It is especially striking how often those who are concerned with the dissemination of research findings substitute a faith that good research will find its audience for systematic understanding into the process of change.

The Role of Knowledge Brokers

Federal research administrators and researchers are frequently isolated from the policy process. Immersed in the research enterprise, they are often unaware of the needs of policy makers, wary or cynical about "politics," and unaccustomed to communicating in nontechnical terms. Frequently there is a similar gulf between researchers and program managers. We noted considerable tension between program officials, who felt they received little help from research, and research administrators, who were weary of anti-intellectual program managers and their demands for how-to-do-it manuals.

The past several years have seen wide use of knowledge brokers in the federal government to bring social scientists and policy makers

[8]See Howard R. Davis and Susan E. Salasin, "Strengthening the Contribution of Social R&D to Policy Making," hereafter cited as Davis and Salasin, "Strengthening Social R&D," in Lynn (1978a).

[9]For an important recent exception, see the RAND study of educational innovation commissioned by the Office of Education, Berman and McLaughlin (1974).

closer together. Knowledge brokers ideally function by dealing, on the one hand, with producers of knowledge, providing information on the needs of policy makers, and, on the other, with policy makers, the users, to whom they provide knowledge from the research community. They can greatly assist in bridging the gaps and breaking down the hostility between researchers, program managers, federal policy makers, and third-party users. In several agencies, research administrators described to us their ties to policy makers in terms of their relationships with the knowledge brokers in the department's planning and policy offices. Knowledge brokers typically are articulate about both research and policy issues, though their sympathies are apt to lie with the policy makers. Although hard to document, our impression is that effective brokerage improves the content of internal departmental and agency communications as well as the relations between researchers and policy makers. In addition, research brokers provide a main line of communication between the departments, the White House, OMB, and Congress.[10]

The Office of the Assistant Secretary for Planning and Evaluation (ASPE) in HEW provides a prime example of a relatively well-institutionalized departmental research brokerage function. The assistant secretary serves as an adviser to the secretary in the innermost circle of the departmental decision-making process. Usually from an academic background, or at least well-respected by the research community, the assistant secretary is aided by a staff with academic training and analytical capabilities. The fiscal and staff resources of the office are primarily devoted to collecting and analyzing data pertaining to social problems that are already acknowledged and accepted, although some portion of their work may be directed toward forecasting and defining future policy or program concerns. ASPE participates in decisions on ongoing programs within the department or new program initiatives, the implementation of policies mandated by Congress or the President, and policy recommendations to Congress or the President generated within the department. Occasionally, a command of specialized knowledge resources casts this office in the role of final arbiter of particular policies or at least gives it substantial veto power (see Seidl and Davis, "Health," *in* Lynn 1978b).

A comparison of the federal government's organization charts of 1965 with those of 1975 shows the rapid institutionalization of research brokerage at the agency and subdivision levels. Central offices of

[10]For a general review of recent developments in knowledge brokerage, see James L. Sundquist, "Research Brokerage: The Weak Link," hereafter cited as Sundquist, "Research Brokerage," *in* Lynn (1978a).

planning and analysis have been created in four major federal departments as part of the drive to implement the Program Planning Budget System (PPBS) throughout government. The Council of Economic Advisers in the Executive Office of the President and the director of Agricultural Economics in the Department of Agriculture are other examples of the institutionalization of knowledge brokerage in the executive branch.

The current use of knowledge brokers, however, is highly varied across the government, primarily because of the varied importance of the planning and policy analysis activities that comprise their major function. Where these activities are influential in decision making, the brokerage function tends to be well developed. There are, however, few federal departments and agencies with strong planning and analysis offices. Where such offices do not exist, the brokerage function or position may exist without real influence and access to the highest policy officials. The success of the brokerage function is therefore largely dependent on how effectively program planning is managed: if there is an orderly policy-planning process, knowledge brokers can channel research information to policy makers and information on policy needs to researchers.

In Congress, the fragmentation of decision making complicates the organization of research brokerage, but also makes it essential. Responsibility for policy and program development is fragmented among numerous committees and subcommittees. To relieve the process of trying to build the necessary analysis and brokerage capacity subcommittee by subcommittee, there has been a move to centralize these functions in support agencies that are politically neutral. Hence, the Congressional Research Service within the Library of Congress, the Office of Technology Assessment, the General Accounting Office, and the Congressional Budget Office are coming to serve the congressional policy maker in a role broadly analogous to that of brokers in the executive branch. The full potential of these organizations to influence and help shape congressional deliberations has yet to be realized.

MANAGING THE SYSTEM

Our background studies focused on three problems of administrative practice that are common to the system of social knowledge production and application: staffing; stability of funding; and the choice of appropriate instruments of research support, an issue that reaches beyond the traditional alternatives of grants and contracts.

Patterns of Staffing

Frequent turnovers among high-level decision makers affect the quality and coherence of programs of social knowledge production and application as well as the morale of other staff members. Indeed, both researchers and program staff frequently observed that research priorities are constantly shifting, agencies are continually being reorganized, and those in leadership posts rarely occupy their positions long enough to develop good working relationships with people in the field. Overall, the lack of stability among high-level departmental and agency officials has caused a serious instability in programs.

Midlevel staffing patterns in agencies that support social knowledge production and application also have significant effects on the way that research programs are funded and managed. In many instances, research administrators are expected to perform broad planning and management functions without adequate staff to do the job. This reflects a far more general difficulty of federal staffing as the government has been given new and expanded responsibilities in recent decades. It is striking to note that, although the overall federal budget has increased dramatically since 1948, the number of federal employees has been remarkably stable.[11]

The consequences of labor-scarce environments are readily apparent in the planning, monitoring, and analysis of knowledge production and application activities, including in-house research.[12] In most cases, the same staff members are responsible for designing and generating new projects and for overseeing ongoing projects. As a result, there appears to be a tradeoff between planning and monitoring functions that tends to leave one or the other neglected. This observation echoes the findings of another committee of the National Research Council, which evaluated the programs of the Office of Manpower Research and Development (OMRD) of the Department of Labor. The committee concluded that constraints on the staffing level of OMRD, imposed by OMB, had caused a decline in competence and left the office incapable of deriving maximum benefit from its R&D expenditures (National Research Council 1975).

Agency monitoring is overly routinized in quarterly and semiannual reporting requirements that are costly and time-consuming for investigators and do not necessarily enhance the quality of project results. In

[11]In 1948 there were slightly more than 2.0 million federal employees; in 1977 there were slightly less than 2.8 million (Office of Management and Budget 1976).

[12]See Richard Collins Davis, "Staffing Patterns in Social R&D Agencies," hereafter cited as R. C. Davis, "Staffing," *in* Glennan (1978).

addition, the effects of staff shortages have resulted in an enforced neglect of the policy implications of the research that is supported and in constraints on the capacity to disseminate research results and to develop or promote practice in the field (see R. C. Davis, "Staffing," *in* Glennan 1978).

Congress and OMB have responded to requests for more adequate staffing by instead prescribing stricter controls to be used by the agencies supporting research. This sort of "controlism" has involved an increasing use of contracts rather than grants, demands for better justification for staff increases, and more attention to Civil Service requirements (see R. C. Davis, "Staffing," *in* Glennan 1978). In general, however, the combined effects of Civil Service restrictions on recruiting and personnel ceilings imposed by OMB have created barriers to filling key staff positions with qualified experts. The length of time needed to hire desirable personnel at higher levels was frequently cited as the reason for having lost prospective employees to other jobs. In many cases, less-qualified personnel have been hired because of Civil Service point preferences and register classifications. Established to ensure equity in federal hiring practices, Civil Service regulations are generally insensitive to the staffing needs of agencies that support social knowledge production and application.

Stability of Funding

Agencies supporting social knowledge production and application frequently are subject to highly uncertain and unstable funding. Erratic and excessive increases and decreases in funding levels distort research management and decision making and jeopardize the coherence and quality of programs. Although sudden budget increases are seldom cited as a problem by research administrators, such increases frequently do create severe management difficulties. We found that the quality and usefulness of research activities suffer if budget resources exceed the capacity of an agency staff to manage them carefully. Because of the inevitable emphasis on spending money before spending authority is lost, decisions concerning which problems should be researched and which investigators should be chosen are made hurriedly and with insufficient care. If staff resources are inadequate, management and monitoring of new projects, as well as of ongoing projects, suffer. Moreover, increased budgets often bring new constituents, who add to the political and bureaucratic pressures on research administrators.

The problems of unscheduled poverty are more familiar. When

sudden funding cutbacks occur, research managers must inevitably make controversial decisions concerning how to distribute the pain. Pressures from researchers, advisory boards, and a variety of constituent groups come into play. Both staff and researcher morale usually deteriorate, and the quality of research management suffers. Rather than causing a reduction in low-priority research, suddenly or sharply imposed cutbacks may jeopardize the coherence and stability of an agency's entire program.[13]

Substantial unexpected funding cutbacks can be particularly detrimental to the management efforts of large agencies; they force the administrative mechanism to halt while the staff do a total replanning that is costly in time and attention. Reductions are also destructive of the innovative efforts of agency staff, who are discouraged by the poor prospect of being able to carry out existing plans.

Overall, uncertainty surrounding the funding levels of agencies supporting social knowledge production and application is detrimental to the quality and usefulness of research products. Seidl and Davis ("Health," *in* Lynn 1978b) identified this uncertainty as a significant problem for several of the agencies responsible for health services research; it discourages strategic planning efforts and contributes to the politically inspired search for the most "salable" research proposals. This, in turn, leads to unrealistically high expectations of agency administrators, as well as of Congress, about project outcomes. When these expectations are dashed, the agency's credibility is jeopardized and further instability results.

Uncertain budgets (and late appropriations) also hamper the awarding of grants and contracts. Requests for proposals and grant announcements take time to prepare, and proposals take time to review. When levels of funding are uncertain, the planning and conduct of competitions are impaired. Moreover, unstable and uncertain patterns of funding are a barrier to long-term commitments with research performers, even when it seems likely that the quality and usefulness of the results would be enhanced by a long-term commitment.

Choosing Instruments of Support

Although some agencies are restricted to grants, for most agencies the choice among alternative instruments of support is a function of research management. Decisions on whether or not a request for proposal (RFP) is to be issued and what it will contain must be made

[13]See the concluding paper by Laurence E. Lynn, Jr., *in* Lynn (1978b).

before investigators are selected. Our management studies sought to identify factors that influence decisions concerning which mechanism—grant or contract—to use. Beyond this, we attempted, though less systematically, to understand the rationale for, and the role of, an intramural research capability.

There is no consistent pattern of grant and contract use throughout the federal government. Some agencies use contracts almost entirely, others rely exclusively on grants, while still others use some mix of the two. Traditionally, grants have been used to provide general support for researchers seeking new knowledge and new methods of obtaining knowledge; they have typically been awarded on the basis of the scientific merit of performer-initiated proposals. Contracts have been used when a sponsor has a specifiable product and wants to hold the performer accountable for producing it; they have been awarded on the basis of cost and responsiveness to agency specifications.[14] The diversity we found, however, cannot be explained by consistent differences in the specificity of the knowledge being sought or in the need to hold researchers accountable to the funding source.

The use of contracts, rather than grants, has increased significantly in recent years, in part in response to OMB and other demands for accountability. Since grants are usually awarded to universities while contracts, especially competitive ones, are typically won by research consulting firms, the increased use of contracts to ensure accountability has fueled the growth of a relatively new performer sector— comprised mainly of for-profit and nonprofit consulting firms—that operates outside the norms and constraints of the academic research community. Indeed, the pressure that the use of contracts has put on the academic community is most clearly seen in the number of university-based researchers who have formed their own consulting firms in order to bid on, win, and execute competitively awarded contracts.

This change in the performer sector has advantages. It has provided access to federal support by many researchers who are outside the traditional university setting and who tend to have a more broadly interdisciplinary and problem-oriented focus. But it has disadvantages as well. The growth of for-profit and nonprofit consulting firms has created significant problems of quality control. Awards are not always made to the most competent firms, largely because the competitive

---

[14]For an elaboration of the historical context for these practices, see Thomas K. Glennan, Jr., and Mark A. Abramson, "Grants and Contracts Policies for Social Research and Development," hereafter cited as Glennan and Abramson, "Grants and Contracts," in Glennan (1978).

bidding process tends to put greater emphasis on skillfully written proposals than on research competence and quality research products. Concern is often voiced about the fraction of total staff time many consulting firms devote to surveying RFPs and writing proposals (see Glennan and Abramson, "Grants and Contracts," *in* Glennan 1978).

Because of recent innovations in research management, the traditional distinctions between grants and contracts are rapidly fading: contracts can be loosely structured and awarded in response to unsolicited proposals; grants can be tightly written with requirements for the delivery of specified products and awarded on the basis of narrowly defined competitions.[15] As support arrangements have become more adaptive, grants and contracts can be used virtually interchangeably. But research administrators vary widely in their awareness of this flexibility (see Glennan and Abramson, "Grants and Contracts," *in* Glennan 1978 and Davis and Hayes, "Early Childhood," *in* Lynn 1978b), and in many agencies standard operating procedure still dictates the choice among alternative instruments of support.

Nevertheless, it would be a mistake to assume that the choice of instruments does not matter: contracts imply a concern for the performer's accountability; grants imply a respect for the performer's autonomy and initiative. The symbolic meaning of these methods can be important in agency–performer communications and to the reputation of the research agency (see Glennan and Abramson, "Grants and Contracts," *in* Glennan 1978). But the crucial need is to reach a sound decision on whether and how planning, problem selection, and research design are to be shared between the supporting agency and the research investigator. Methods of support can then be flexibly adapted to these decisions.

Our study did not include a systematic investigation of the intramural research capabilities of agencies that support social knowledge production and application, but we believe that such a capability offers several advantages in the case of research meant to address specified program or policy needs. In-house researchers tend to understand the needs and priorities of an agency better than outsiders do. When research is done externally, the definition of problems to be researched and the design of work to be undertaken seem to fall entirely either to the funder or to the investigator. When research is done in-house, there is often better communication and coordination between those who might use the results of the work and those who perform it. Hence, an intramural research capability can enhance the likelihood of an agency's using the

[15]See Linda Ingram, "The 'Best' Social Research: Who Does It and Who Funds It?," *in* Lynn (1978b).

results of the research it supports. Indeed, when knowledge production and application activities are conducted in-house, there is a greater tendency on the part of agency decision makers to regard them as a legitimate and valuable part of ongoing administrative activities and programs. We have found this to be true of the Social Security Administration, NIMH, and the Department of Agriculture's Economic Research Service, the primary supporters of intramural knowledge production and application activities (see Seidl and Davis, "Health," *in* Lynn 1978b).

Our review of instruments of support again highlighted the extent to which administrators focus on individual research projects rather than on programs of research or on broad knowledge production efforts. The heart of the research management process is committing funds, and this task typically revolves around decisions concerning the support of individual projects. This focus is to some degree inevitable: research projects are the research administrator's units of work, for which he or she can be held specifically accountable. They have a reality and meaning that the cumulative result of many pieces of research performed at different times and in different places may not.

Although research administrators are typically project-oriented, we did find a few instances of support for broader programs of research, including cooperative agreements between research agencies and performer institutions, program announcements and priorities statements, and research programs shaped by strong direction. It is clearly possible to depart from the pattern of project-by-project decision making, although it is seldom done (see Katz, "Survey Methodology," *in* Stokes 1978). The most significant departures are the few instances in which agencies have provided level-of-effort funding to problem-oriented research institutions. The Air Force's Project RAND and federal grants to create and sustain the Urban Institute and the Institute for Research on Poverty are examples of efforts to support research in broad problem areas over relatively long periods of time. Most of the evidence of our study, however, pointed to the systematic discouragement and erosion of this method of support by federal management and budget officials, as well as by policy analysis and program development offices. With their "what has this study done for me" orientation, most of these officials regard institutional support, which has longer time horizons and a broader problem focus, with suspicion or active hostility. Hence, funding agencies have given little attention to the potential of such arrangements in the recent past.

CONCLUSIONS

Our detailed studies of the system of federal support for social knowledge production and application reinforce the evidence of the decentralized character of the system. A vast array of departments, agencies, bureaus, offices, and divisions support research and development activities on a variety of interrelated social problems. The principal findings of our studies of how the system is organized and managed can be grouped in three broad clusters: setting research agendas, disseminating and applying results, and managing the system.

Setting research agendas is a largely reactive process, and examples of systematic planning are rare. Although there is almost no duplication of research effort between agencies, there are very few cases of agencies with overlapping responsibilities establishing research priorities through coordinated planning. Hence, there are important problems that fall in the gaps between agencies, and little attention is given to identifying and planning research on emerging problems. The incentives for planning are generally weak and inconsistent.

More effective application of knowledge is hampered by doubts as to the quality or relevance of research, the lack of developed policies on the dissemination and use of research findings, and little sense of the appropriate audience for particular research results. An excessive focus on the results of individual projects discourages synthesis of knowledge from several projects or other sources. Research administrators have a limited understanding of how new information can foster innovation and change. The recent past has seen a wider use of knowledge brokers in the federal government to bridge the gap between policy makers and the research community.

The management of the system is handicapped by the rapid turnover of leadership at the highest level of government and by arbitrary staff ceilings and unresponsive hiring policies for agencies that support social knowledge production and application. Uncertainties of funding are a pervasive problem; the quality of a research program can be harmed by unforeseen prosperity as well as by unscheduled poverty. The choice of instruments of support is too often a matter of standard operating procedure that fails to take advantage of the flexibility available to the research administrator and to press the possibility of supporting programs with longer time perspectives and a broader problem focus.

4 Perspectives on Federal Support for Knowledge Production and Application

Our review of the budget and management of federal support in Chapters 2 and 3 facilitates a greater understanding of the current system and the ways it might be improved. Some of the recommendations in Chapter 5 flow from findings already presented; indeed, some are implied by the language we have used. But our review also gave us some fresh perspectives on the links of research to action on social problems and the diversity of the federal investment in social knowledge. Hence, this chapter presents a new way of thinking about the system of federal support—about the diversity of the federal role, the linkage of research to government, and the audience for social knowledge production and application—before we present our recommendations in Chapter 5.

THE NATURE OF GOVERNMENT

Three major characteristics of government create much of the difficulty in linking research and the policy process: the necessarily political character of government; the need for government to act on incomplete information; and the short time perspective typical in government. Understanding these characteristics is important in developing recommendations for strengthening the system of federal support for the production and application of knowledge of social problems.

54

The Political Character of Government

The policy process in government is inherently political. There is no disparagement in this observation; on the contrary, the policy process legitimately resolves conflicts among competing interests. If stabilizing farm income requires higher food prices in the marketplace, the trade-off between the two requires a political judgment. Only a political process can legitimately make that judgment.

Conflicts are present in all policy areas, but they are especially marked in social policy. Indeed, a problem tends to be called "social" if there are sharp conflicts among interests or values. Putting a man on the moon could be seen as overwhelmingly a technological problem, but "the problem of our cities," which also has a large technological component, is far more likely to be seen as a social issue, because of the conflicting interests and values that are involved.

Government decisions on the support and application of research are not exempt from the political process. Research administrators, a critical subcommunity of government, live in a very political environment; most federal research programs are deeply enmeshed in bureaucratic, special interest, and legislative politics. There are numerous and diverse pressures on research managers from sources such as departmental officials, OMB and the White House, congressional committees, and organized interest groups.

These pressures, detailed in our management studies (Glennan 1978, Lynn 1978b), lead to knowledge production and application activities in a variety of political contexts.

- R&D programs have been started as symbolic acts intended to demonstrate national concern for particular social problems. The activities recently initiated in the Alcohol, Drug Abuse, and Mental Health Administration on rape and its prevention and on the family and television violence were intended to demonstrate national concern for important social problems.
- R&D activities have been undertaken as a means of initiating a reform when there is no consensus on a proposed program. Thus, the income maintenance experiments were undertaken after an initiative toward a national income maintenance program was turned aside by President Johnson. More recently, a senator succeeded in leading Congress to adopt legislation providing resources for a large experiment with housing allowances—after failing to persuade his colleagues to institute a national housing allowance program.
- R&D activities have sometimes been a compromise between

political opponents who are unable to resolve their differences. The current evaluation of compensatory education programs by the National Institute of Education was agreed to by competing congressional factions seeking to change the formula for the distribution of compensatory education funds.

• R&D activities have been initiated to provide grounds for delaying action. This is true of current efforts to examine the effects of various requirements of the proposed Federal Interagency Child Care Standards. Sometimes, program evaluations are initiated to forestall large increases in funding for politically popular programs.

• R&D programs have been initiated when the federal government is kept from taking direct action by the division of functions among levels of government. Federally funded R&D in education has been aimed at goals, such as improving programs for the disadvantaged or training future scientists, that the federal government cannot pursue directly because responsibility for education lies with the states and their local units of government.

In contrast to the policy process, research is inherently apolitical in the sense that it cannot resolve the value conflicts at the heart of the policy process. Research may clarify these differences and widen or narrow the area of disagreement by showing the likely consequences of policy choices, but research cannot show why one set of values or interests should be preferred to another.

There is no way to depoliticize the support of research and the use of its results, but effective strategies for acquiring and using research results can take account of the political nature of the policy process. There must be effective political support both for the production of knowledge on social problems and for its application by governmental and other users.

The Need to Act on Incomplete Information

Related to the political character of government is its need to act on incomplete information. Evidence about the nature of social problems or the consequences of alternative social policies will never be exhaustive. Those who reach decisions through the policy process should—indeed must—make decisions on limited information.

The need to act on incomplete information is unavoidable and is not simply the result of neglect in building an information base for action. In fact, attempts to strengthen such a base are more likely to succeed if there is a realistic understanding of what research cannot do. Government deals with extraordinarily complex social problems, and any major policy will be based on many assumptions about individual or group behavior. Research can increase knowledge about the validity of those assumptions, but it can never confirm them all.

This can be illustrated by some of the recent large-scale social experiments undertaken by government. The income maintenance experiments in New Jersey and Pennsylvania were a major assault on a key question about a "negative income tax" plan: whether poor people with jobs would go on working if a negative income tax gave them a guaranteed minimum income. The experiment was designed to see whether the members of several hundred poor families, chosen randomly in five cities, would stop working when they were eligible for a negative income tax. Few did.

But many uncertainties remained. Did the result depend on special characteristics of the experimental situation? Since this was a small sample, neighboring families were rarely enrolled: would the responses have differed if the plan were universal and publicly advertised? The participants knew the experiment would last only three years: would their behavior have been different if this had been a permanent program? The experiment was carried out in small cities: would the effect have been different in other types of communities?

Questions such as these are now being explored in experiments that have followed the initial effort in New Jersey. For example, part of the experiment with housing allowances being supported by the Department of Housing and Urban Development involves an entire city, which may make a critical additional contribution to what is known. But the need to act on incomplete evidence will remain. If the federal government were to try to study all of the factors in this and other social programs, the research capacity of the country would soon be swamped and the government would lose the will to act.

This reality leads to a further observation of considerable importance: since research is a limited resource, effective strategies of social knowledge production and application should consider the ways it can count most. Knowledge based on good research can be costly, and the research community at any time has a limited capacity to produce it. Investments in research should therefore be based on an understanding of the diversified ways that knowledge obtained from this investment can strengthen the nation's capacity to see and deal with its social problems.

The Time Perspective of Government

A third characteristic of the policy process is its short time perspective, a perspective much briefer than the life of major social issues. This is partly a matter of the brief tenure of office of leading participants. The average stay of cabinet secretaries is about two years; the average of undersecretaries and assistant secretaries is even shorter. The short time perspective is also partly due to constitutional and statutory constraints. The biennial cycle of elections is uppermost in the minds of members of Congress, especially representatives; sessions of Congress are briefer still. The budget process, which controls many of the planning and evaluative efforts of government, still follows an annual cycle.

For these reasons, the time perspective of policy makers is short. Their demands for knowledge are often immediate. Policy does not wait for relevant knowledge to become available. Under the pressure of events and constituencies, legislation is passed, programs started, regulations and guidelines written, and funds authorized, appropriated, and spent—whether or not relevant analysis and research findings are in place. Indeed, the process often operates in reverse. The systematic accumulation of knowledge on a scale appropriate to a problem may not begin until policies and programs are enacted. Once in operation, new programs legitimize the large-scale expenditure of funds for research. This was true, for example, of research on health care, which followed the enactment of Medicare and Medicaid legislation in the 1960s. The same was true of research on income maintenance, environmental protection, and energy development.

But if the time perspective of the policy process is short, the life expectancy of major social problems is not. Very few of the problems of our society are solved in a single season or by a single action; on the contrary, policies to deal with them are fashioned incrementally over time in a series of partial measures. And as perceptions of a problem change over time, so do policy solutions. For example, the federal role in the financing of health care for the poor has been debated for four decades: important steps, including the Kerr-Mills Act, Medicaid, and Medicare, have been taken, but the debate goes on and further developments are virtually certain. And the importance of the turnover of participants in the policy process should not be exaggerated; the careers of some members of Congress and civil servants are as long-lived as the social problems they face. Members of key congressional committees or subcommittees may hold their posts for many years.

These observations suggest that effective strategies for the production and application of knowledge will need to have varied time perspectives. Some production and application of knowledge should be able to respond to the very short-run needs of government. But the brief cycles of the policy process can be seen as epicycles within a much broader movement of social problems through the stages of recognition, debate, and partial solution over a period of years or decades. Longer perspectives open the possibility of also supporting lines of research that require longer time for a significant return.

Research needs time. Even a next research step into the unknown will take some time; more ambitious ventures will require more time, and the amount will be harder to predict. The development of a research-based understanding of social problems may be the product of many studies over many years, or even decades, rather than of a few studies in a year or two. In particular, research on changes in individual or group behavior may require a long time. Years are needed to find the answers to such questions as the effect of lower prices on medical care utilization or the effect of a guaranteed minimum income on participation in the labor force. If one traces the length of time it takes to develop the ideas and methods that underlie a particular program of research, an even longer time horizon emerges. For example, the models that were deployed in the negative income tax experiments evolved out of a generation of theoretical and empirical work by economists concerned with labor force behavior.[1] The sample designs used in these experiments were based on statistical concepts developed over the previous three decades.

Short-run, event-forced policy making may keep the value of long-term research from being recognized. The current participants in the policy process, whose predecessors did not leave them with a firm base of information, are understandably preoccupied with their immediate information needs rather than with laying a firmer base for their successors. The farther in the future the results of research, the smaller its current constituency. Policy making is concerned with current issues and problems. Policy makers with short time horizons would rather commit resources to obtain immediate help than invest in an uncertain future in which they may play no part. The need to devise ways of supporting longer-term research is therefore an unresolved issue of the federal investment in knowledge of social problems.

A recognition of the tensions between the policy making and the research process has helped to reorganize our thinking about linking government and research. Better policies and institutional arrangements are needed to balance the inherently political, event-forced, short-run perspectives of the policy process with a research process that needs political support, the effective deployment of a scarce resource, and time.

---

[1] See W. Joseph Heffernan, Jr., "Social Science Research and the Articulation of a Negative Income Tax Policy," hereafter cited as Heffernan, "Negative Income Tax," *in* Stokes (1978).

DIVERSITY IN THE FEDERAL INVESTMENT

A key to this balance is diversity in the federal investment in knowledge of social problems. There is more diversity in the present investment than is commonly recognized, and it is useful to describe more clearly the extent and nature of the variation. We believe that an explicit portfolio approach—matching different policies to different types of investment—can strengthen the system of federal support.

To describe more clearly the diversity of the present system, we have found it useful to think of a support-and-application "loop" that is closed when research supported with federal funds leads to knowledge that is applied by governmental or nongovernmental users. This loop has two arcs, one representing the setting of research agendas and the support of the work, the other representing the dissemination and application of the knowledge gained by research. There is remarkable variety in support-and-application loops—in the length of time needed to close the loop, in how easily applications can be foreseen when the research is supported, and in the range of application a line of research will yield.

This variety was evident in the work examined by our background studies. In some of the federally supported studies prompted by policy or program needs, there are close ties between the planning and support of research, on the one hand, and the application of its results, on the other. If the Social Security Administration wants to improve its estimate of the number of people who will continue to work rather than draw benefits after the age at which they are entitled to social security, it launches a study of movements into and out of payment status and uses the results in its actuarial calculations.

But in other research, especially studies that are intended to gain a broader understanding of social problems or to expand the basic knowledge or methods of social science, the ties between support and application may be much longer-term and varied and difficult to forecast. A study of the rise of modern demography noted that the mathematical studies of self-renewal in human and other populations, which were carried out before and after the First World War, formulated equilibrium models of population increase that allow the interconnections of age composition, fertility, and mortality to be spelled out.[2]

But it was not until after the Second World War that this work was used by demographers to devise methods for drawing sound inferences

[2]See Frank W. Notestein, "A Partial View of the Development of American Demography in the Late 1960s," hereafter cited as Notestein, "Demography," *in* Stokes (1978).

from the very defective data of many less developed countries. This work did much to alert both the United States government and the governments of the nations involved to the great potential for rapid population growth in the less developed world with its attendant need for food, governmental services, and productive equipment. Realization of the scope of these needs has been the most important factor fostering the policies designed to reduce human fertility that have been adopted by governments ruling more than three-quarters of the population in the less developed world. The same work, of course, underlies in a sense much of the methodological advance that has permitted an understanding of the ways in which changed fertility and mortality in the United States will affect social and economic life in future decades. The eventual return from the investment in the original work was substantial, but the varied loops of support and application followed long and uncertain paths before they were closed.

The distinction between these cases, once it is explicit, may seem obvious, yet the tendency to overlook it blurs current discussion of federal policy on the support and application of research on social problems. This is starkly evident if one considers the extraordinarily varied meanings of "policy relevance." All of the following tests are at times associated with the term by those who use it:[3]

- Have the findings of this research helped to solve the problem to which it is directed?
- Have the findings of this research been incorporated into social policies or programs intended to ameliorate the problem?
- Have the findings of this research been analyzed and discussed by someone influential in the policy process?
- Are the findings of this research potentially relevant to a current policy debate?
- Are the findings of this research potentially relevant to future policy debates?
- Has this research shed light on the nature of a social problem or condition or on how society or its members function?
- Has this research contributed to the formulation, design, and conduct of other research, the findings of which will be helpful in the making of current or future policy?
- Does this research advance an intellectual discipline that may help to ameliorate social problems?

[3]This variety is a major theme of our companion essays on policy relevance. These tests are drawn from Laurence E. Lynn, Jr., "The Question of Relevance," *in* Lynn (1978a).

• Does this research have scientific merit in the opinion of qualified social scientists?

These varied meanings of "policy relevance" reflect different links between the production and application of knowledge. We believe that an appreciation of such differences can help in framing policies that will bring knowledge more effectively to bear on social problems.

The key to these differences is the length, predictability, and singleness of the loop of knowledge production and application that links the initial support of research with its eventual use. In the study of those entitled to payments under the social security system, a single loop between production and application was clearly foreseen and immediately closed. But in the studies of population renewal, the multiple links between the first mathematical models and the applications to public policy were very long run and very largely unforeseen. Indeed, in the latter case, the original work was for a considerable period almost completely forgotten.

These differences can also be described by whether the information sought by research, and applied from research, is in a given period the same. In the social security example, the answer was yes: the government saw what it needed and procured and applied it—all in a brief interval. In the demographic example, the answer was no: the scientific knowledge applied by our own government, by other governments, by international agencies, and by many private organizations and individuals had been produced years before its use; the eventual users played no part in the original investment. And today, the federal government continues to support basic demographic research that may lead to further applications in future years.

LINKAGE MODELS

In light of these differences—in the length, predictability, and multiplicity of the loops between the production and use of knowledge of social problems—we can characterize knowledge production and application activities by their immediate purposes: program-supporting, policy-forming, problem-exploring, or knowledge-building. For each of these four immediate purposes of knowledge production and knowledge application activities, we can describe a linkage model that has important implications for the way the support and application loops should be conceived and managed.

Program-Supporting

In the first model, information is sought to fill clearly understood requirements of an operating social program. The length of time between the beginning of the research and the use of the results may be measured in weeks or months, or at most a few years, and it is often quite clear in the planning stage how the information from research will be combined with other program data, disseminated to intended users, and applied.

For example, the Urban Mass Transportation Administration (UMTA) funds a variety of program-supporting activities supporting its mission of improving public transportation services. In fiscal 1976, UMTA spent over $4 million in research on such questions as:

• What are the economic, environmental, and performance factors that may affect the acceptance of "automated guideway transit" systems in urban areas?

• What are the alternative means of financing public transportation capital expenses?

UMTA also spent more than $9 million in fiscal 1976 in support of demonstration projects to test and promote innovative uses of transit services. In addition to these kinds of research and demonstration efforts, UMTA funds a variety of dissemination activities aimed at providing state and local planners with the latest technology in transit planning tools.

Policy-Forming

In this model of linkage, information is sought from research to assist in making policy. Our survey of federal spending found a very wide range of social research activities for this purpose, including studies that were meant to feed information into policy making on health, education, employment and training, income security, economic growth, transportation, housing, law enforcement, and energy.

Although the program-supporting and policy-forming models of linkage are much alike, the loops in the policy-forming model tend to be longer, more multiple, and less predictable. There would be fewer uncertainties of support and application if policy making were concerned only with finding policy means to agreed-upon ends. But for politically sensitive policies, the conduct and results of research as well as its possible uses may be controversial. It is therefore reasonable to classify as "policy-forming" research that may provide information to the policy process, whether or not the loop of support and application is actually closed.

Problem-Exploring

In the third model of linkage, which is outside the most familiar conceptions of the role of social R&D, research seeks to understand a social problem without starting from any well-defined program or policy needs. The immediate goal is to characterize a social problem, to try to understand its nature and causes, and to find possible points of intervention in dealing with it. In the middle or longer run, such exploration can bring a substantial return as new policies are developed and new programs launched, but it is not clear at the beginning how and when the support and application loop will be closed.

Understanding this model helps to clarify both an aspect of current research and a goal of the social R&D system. We found that a good deal of the activities currently funded by mission (operating) agencies is better described as an effort to develop knowledge of a problem than as an effort to develop policy or meet program requirements. For example, the studies of global interdependence funded by the Department of State's Office of External Research seek to understand the web of relationships that tie this country to the rest of the world. And the studies of behavioral factors in highway accidents funded by the Department of Transportation's National Highway Traffic Safety Administration seek to understand why people drive unsafely—without beginning from specific policy or program goals.

This type of research can be more easily recognized if the funding agency is not aligned with a program or policy office. The productivity studies sponsored by NSF, the crime and delinquency research of NIMH, and the population studies of the National Institute of Child Health and Development are all examples of problem-exploring efforts supported by research agencies. Each of these seeks to understand a problem rather than to respond to immediate policy or program demands, although each may yield longer-term policy or program returns.

Some of the most significant examples of problem exploration result from special commissions or inquiries that span the interests of many federal agencies. One example is federally supported research on poverty. As concern about the poor grew in the 1960s, it was clear that we knew surprisingly little about who was poor and why. It was therefore felt to be important to develop a firmer understanding through research. The resulting studies over a decade and a half have provided a sharper definition of poverty and a clearer insight into its causes. It is now known, for example, how many of the poor are children in homes headed by females who have little prospect of entering the labor force; or are members of families in which the wage earner works full time but at a subsistence wage; or are temporarily poor because of short-term changes in income or in family needs.

Although this gain in understanding was not prompted by immediate policy needs, it has helped to shape the terms of the policy debate. The early plans for the "War on Poverty" placed a heavy emphasis on manpower training and education. Yet the emerging studies of the poor showed that these programs could do little to improve the condition of children in single-parent homes or of workers close to their earning potential at low wages and were often irrelevant to the needs of the temporarily poor. Indeed, these findings encouraged the alternative view that some form of income maintenance should be a fundamental part of national policy. Accordingly, President Johnson in 1968 appointed an Income Maintenance Commission, which moved toward a negative income tax as a desirable form of income maintenance policy. Later, President Nixon proposed the Family Assistance Plan, which also owed a good deal to research. The impact of varied formulations of the Family Assistance Plan was projected by models developed by the Income Maintenance Commission and later refined by work sponsored by the Social Security Administration and the Office of Economic Opportunity.

Although the Family Assistance Plan failed in Congress, a base of understanding of poverty continued to be developed. Later studies clarified the overlapping effects of an array of income security programs, such as welfare, food stamps, and unemployment insurance. They also enlarged what was known about movements into, and out of, poverty status. In the early 1970s the findings from this widening stream of research led the secretary of HEW to support an income supplement program developed by the staff of the assistant secretary for planning and evaluation. Although this proposal also failed, research on poverty had again helped to shape the policy debate.

Several points can be made about this example of problem exploration. The effort was prompted initially by the goal of understanding a significant social problem. Much of the work was shaped by researchers who were brought into contact with policy makers but given substantial freedom to develop their research. A major, problem-centered research organization, the Institute for Research on Poverty at the University of Wisconsin, was created to help focus the research effort, and a series of grants and contracts built up an important research capability on poverty in several other organizations. Although there was direct involvement of researchers in the development of policy, the understanding gained from research entered the policy process largely through intervening knowledge brokers.

A second major example of problem exploration is the work of the (Murphy) Commission on the Organization of the Government for the Conduct of Foreign Policy. In this case, a joint presidential–congressional commission had an explicit policy mandate: to recommend ways of strengthening the organization of the foreign affairs sector of the federal government. But the larger significance of the commission's work will almost certainly be its background studies. Indeed, the tensions between the Executive and Congress sharply limited the direct policy yield of the commission. The then-majority leader of the Senate, who as a sponsor and member of the commission was deeply disappointed by its limited policy yield, described its recommendations as "a very thin gruel served up in a very thick cup." But the commission is likely to have a delayed and indirect effect as future policy makers absorb, without in some cases knowing the source, its way of looking at such questions as the requirements of decision making under stress, the possibility of detaching foreign policy advocacy from departmental interest, and the role of personnel development in modernizing the organization of the foreign affairs sector. Such an effect is already evident in the reorganization proposals of the Carter Administration.

Knowledge-Building

In the last of the linkage models, the support and application loop is long, highly multiple, and difficult to predict: research is undertaken to enlarge the basic stock of social knowledge—without reference to a problem, to policy alternatives, or to the needs of operating social programs. In the years since the Second World War the federal government has assumed a major share of the nation's investment in activities for knowledge building. This investment is made largely through NSF, NIMH, and several other independent research agencies.

The way this investment has strengthened the government's capacity to recognize, understand, and deal with major social problems is the subject of one of our series of background studies (Stokes 1978). The nation has gotten far more than knowledge for its own sake from this investment in basic advances in the social sciences, as it has gotten far more than pure knowledge from its investment in basic advances in physical or biological knowledge (see Comroe and Dripps 1976).

As in other fields of science, the multiple loops that connect the support and eventual application of the knowledge gained from basic advances in the social sciences are typically long and difficult to forecast, as the example of the early work on population renewal suggests. Hence, they are a natural target of the skepticism of those who would support only social research that promises early results. But the test of quick and foreseeable return would rule out a good deal of research that will be of genuine social benefit in the longer run. Much of the fundamental work in demography would have failed to attract support if direct policy relevance, or even problem relevance, had been the test. But that work has, in the long run, helped us to see and to begin to cope with the problem of population increase on a global scale (Notestein, "Demography," *in* Stokes 1978).

A great many individual studies, including a number that prove to be ill-conceived but productive in their errors, make up the long and uncertain pathways that lead from basic advances of knowledge to the varied applications of those advances. In view of this, it may be fruitless to apply a test of usefulness to individual projects. It would be better to apply a test of scientific value, knowing that significant gains in knowledge will result in the long run. The experience of the physical and biological sciences has shown that well-conceived and sustained programs of basic research tend ultimately to be successful despite the failure of many individual projects and that some of these programs also have substantial social utility.

Indeed, those who want to improve the social utility of basic advances in social science may be mistaken in focusing so much of their attention on criteria for the support of research, in view of the difficulty of knowing in advance how a field of knowledge will develop. It may be far more useful to focus on application, to seek better means of synthesizing and applying to current problems the knowledge that has cumulated from past research.

The failure to distinguish among different linkage models—to see in particular that the criteria of support that are appropriate to activities for program support or policy formation may be quite inappropriate to activities whose purpose is problem exploration or knowledge building—seems to us to underlie some of the tension between Congress and the federal agencies that fund basic research in social science. The congressional hearings of recent years in which NSF has sought to justify its support of basic research are filled with instances of

NSF and its critics talking past each other as each implicitly focused on quite different models of the production and use of knowledge.

AUDIENCE

We will introduce one other element into this framework for thinking about the nation's portfolio of investments in social knowledge production and application: audience. Much of the discussion of how social R&D could be made more "policy relevant" is pervaded by the view that the federal government is itself the prime consumer of the information being developed. But any assumption of this sort is quickly suspect as one considers activities outside the program-supporting and policy-forming models of linkage. Activities to explore problems and build knowledge have multiple audiences, and many of these lie outside the federal government (although it is also true that more can be done to create an audience in government for knowledge that cumulates in the research community). And, as it became abundantly clear in the course of our project, third parties are also meant to benefit from many of the shorter-term loops of social knowledge production and application. The immediate needs of state governments, of local police forces and school systems, of hospitals, farmers, and other groups and individuals are meant to be served by a good deal of the research that we classified as program supporting or policy forming. As noted in Chapter 2, roughly half of all activities aimed at program support, policy formation, and problem exploration are directed to users outside the federal government.

It is important to distinguish different audiences in considering ways of strengthening the system of federal support for social knowledge production and application. Quite different policies may be required to provide for the immediate needs of program managers and policy makers within the federal government, for the needs of well-defined users outside the federal government, and for the future needs of those who prove to be the beneficiaries of research exploring social problems or enlarging our stock of basic social knowledge.

CONCLUSIONS

An awareness of the tensions between the policy process and research has shaped our thinking about linking government and research. The political character of government implies that effective strategies for acquiring and using research-based knowledge need to take account of the political nature of the policy process. There must be effective political support both for the production of knowledge on social problems and for its application by governmental and nongovernmental users.

The need of government to act on incomplete information implies that effective strategies of social knowledge production and application should consider the ways that research, as a costly and limited resource, can count most. Investments in research should be based on an understanding of the diversified ways that the knowledge obtained from this investment can strengthen the nation's capacity to understand and deal with its social problems.

The differing time frames of the policy process and of major social problems imply that effective strategies for the production and application of knowledge will need to have varied time perspectives. Some research and utilization of research knowledge must be able to respond to the very short-run needs of the policy process, but the longer life expectancy of major social problems opens the possibility of investing in research that requires longer time for a significant return. The need to devise ways of supporting such longer-term research is an unresolved issue of federal investment in knowledge of social problems.

The variety of the links between support and application suggests the value of a portfolio approach to the federal investment in knowledge of social problems. Since the system of federal support is supposed to accomplish several quite different things, there should be several quite different investments in the federal research portfolio. Different criteria should be used to manage each, and different returns should be expected from each. More effective policies and institutional arrangements can be devised if the value of such diversity is accepted.

5 Strengthening the System of Federal Support

The current system of federal support of social knowledge production and application has three dominant characteristics:

- It is radically decentralized. The federal government acquired its role in social research and development largely as an adjunct to its broad array of social programs. Most expenditures for social knowledge production and application are mission-oriented, and the management of the system is compartmentalized among scores of agencies.
- It must cope with inherent tensions between the policy and research processes. If government and the research community are to be effectively linked, a policy process that is unavoidably political, incompletely informed, and forced by events must be reconciled with a research process that is unable to resolve value conflicts, resistant to closure, and time consuming.
- It has multiple objectives. The federal government holds a diversified portfolio of investments in social knowledge production and application. It will need very different policies to manage the investments that are meant to improve federal programs and policies, to benefit third parties, to gain more understanding of social problems, and to add basic resources of knowledge and method.

The detailed information gained from our studies of the present system is an important part of our conclusions. We have increasingly felt

70

that, quite apart from the value of our recommendations, we could render a service by giving a coherent account of the present system.

Nonetheless, we conclude our report with recommendations for strengthening the system. We do so with some hesitancy, since the diversity of the system bars simple remedies. Sweeping organizational prescriptions are more likely to change government than to improve it. We believe that across-the-board reforms, such as the centralization of research administration, the mandated use of peer review or user panels, a shift to multiyear funding, or the establishment of standardized planning processes or standardized formats and procedures for reporting research results would do more harm than good.

We are also alert to the problem of incentives for change as we suggest improvements. The present system is an integral part of ongoing political and administrative processes and so will not easily change. We have therefore sought to devise modifications that recognize the incentives and disincentives that shape the current system.

THE ROLE OF OVERSIGHT

The segmented character of the system of federal support creates an urgent need for effective oversight. Because social knowledge production and application activities are compartmentalized, both within and among federal departments and agencies, the government has generated little systematic research on problems or issues that cut across the jurisdictions and professional perspectives of individual agencies. Furthermore, few attempts are made to bring different agencies together into cooperative, mutually reinforcing research enterprises. And little attention is paid to resource allocation, management, or evaluation of results in contexts larger than individual offices and projects. In short, there is little effective oversight of the knowledge production and application activities supported by the federal government.

A number of institutions in Congress and the executive branch have responsibilities that cut across the interests of individual agencies, permitting them to exercise oversight of at least part of the system of federal support. Within the executive branch, such institutions include OMB; the science adviser to the President and the Office of Science and Technology Policy; and the primary staff offices in the office of the secretary or administrator of each major federal department or agency. In Congress, such institutions include the appropriations committees and subcommittees with responsibility for the major social programs; the authorization committees and subcommittees with major responsibility for social programs; the science and technology oversight committees; the committees on government operations; and certain of the special review arms of Congress, especially the General Accounting Office and the Office of Technology Assessment. The budget committees of Congress and the Congressional Budget Office might also be added to the list.

Effective oversight is consistent with an emerging trend toward the incorporation of more cross-cutting perspectives in the political process. Increasing recognition of the relative scarcity both of federal budgetary and managerial resources and of the nation's natural, economic, and human resources is creating an increased awareness of the need to identify policy and program trade-offs and to consider long-term implications when making policy decisions. Passage of the National Environmental Policy Act, the creation of the Office of Technology Assessment, the growing level of expenditures for program evaluation, the passage and successful implementation of the Federal Budget and Impoundment Control Act, and the popularity and use of the Brookings Institution's *Setting National Priorities* series are evidence of this awareness.

This trend has significant implications for federal support of social knowledge production and application for two reasons. First, it increases the incentive for institutions with a cross-cutting role in policy making to promote investments in new knowledge that will help them in making or recommending policy and program choices, enhancing their influence in the policy process. Second, because of their jurisdictions, these institutions are peculiarly able to promote the kinds of improvements in federal support of social knowledge production and application that we suggest. They are able to maintain direct lines of communication with decision makers, research administrators, and researchers. Most of these institutions have an analytical capacity and participate in the policy-making process. Hence they have both the competence and the opportunity to bridge gaps between decision makers and knowledge producers. And their incentive to perform this role is increasing.

Our recommendations set out a number of ways policy or practice can be strengthened—by the action both of those who operate the system of federal support and of those who can exercise effective oversight. These are grouped under the three broad headings we have used to analyze the existing system: setting research agendas; synthesizing, disseminating, and applying knowledge; and managing the system.

SETTING RESEARCH AGENDAS

To organize social knowledge production activities, federal agencies must establish research priorities, stimulate the interest and involvement of researchers, choose researchers, and commit funds. We have found that the manner in which agencies carry out these tasks is largely ad hoc and reactive. There is little systematic planning of research priorities within goal-oriented frameworks. Moreover, there is too little awareness of the varied requirements of the different types of activities described by the linkage models in Chapter 4.

Planning Research Programs

Frequently the focus and the direction of an agency's research agenda simply emerge from the selection of particular projects and the support of particular investigators; we believe that planning and establishing research priorities should be a distinct and conscious aspect of the administrative processes of agencies that support social knowledge production and application activities.

1.1 We recommend that federal research administrators and oversight officials in departmental policy planning and analysis offices and in the Office of Management and Budget devote more attention and resources to the development of systematic planning processes as a distinct aspect of the support function. These processes should take account of the differences among the types of activities required to improve federal policies or programs, to serve the needs of users outside the government, to explore broad problem areas, and to build new resources of knowledge or method.

Agendas for Program-Supporting and Policy-Forming Activities

The setting of agendas for research that is intended to assist the operation of social programs or to help form social policy should be closely coordinated with program and policy planning. Departments and agencies should be strongly encouraged by OMB and other oversight agencies to establish an explicit management process that connects program and policy planning to the planning of knowledge production and application activities. These connections should build into the planning of research agendas a strong sense of the program or policy audience of the results of the research. The planning of research intended to assist in forming social policy may need to relate the goals of several agencies or departments. The active involvement of oversight officials at the departmental, presidential, or congressional level is in these cases essential.

1.2 We recommend that the users of program-supporting and policy-forming research be more closely involved in setting research agendas. Agency decision makers should have greater input in the planning of program-supporting activities. Policy makers at the departmental and presidential levels and in Congress should have greater input in planning policy-forming research.

Agendas for Problem-Exploring Activities

We strongly encourage agencies to plan broader programs of problem-exploring research. But the compartmentalization of research management in a set of mission agencies often acts as a barrier to designing a research effort that cuts across the interests of a number of agencies or is within the clear province of none. Setting agendas for problem-exploring research is often a task beyond the means of a single agency.

Developing a research-based understanding of problems that transcend the pattern of mission agencies has two related aspects: the need to coordinate the setting of research agendas by several agencies that share a common problem interest; and the need to build an adequate agenda when the problem is poorly matched to the interest of any agency. The latter need is especially marked in the case of a developing problem that may become urgent in the future.

1.3 We recommend more extensive use by oversight institutions of special means to develop adequate research agendas on major social problems that are not well matched to agency missions. These should include the creation of task forces, temporary commissions, and conferences to frame research agendas and the sponsorship of state-of-the-art surveys of existing knowledge related to specified problem areas.

The lead in such efforts could be taken by a number of oversight institutions. In some cases the lead might be taken by a committee or subcommittee of Congress; in others by the science adviser to the President or OMB; in still others by a major department or one of the independent R&D agencies, such as NSF. In the case of the most important social problems that transcend the agency structure, the lead should be taken by the President or by Congress as a whole through the creation of independent, temporary commissions.

The purpose of such commissions would be to review and synthesize knowledge in broad problem areas, to set priorities for future research in these areas, and to explore points of intervention for framing remedial policies or programs. They would be able to mobilize unusual expertise for one or several years to enlarge understanding of a broad problem area and stimulate problem-exploring research. Although presidential and presidential-congressional commissions do not have an outstanding reputation of achievement in influencing policy, they have an impressive record in redefining problems and in focusing future research. The backup volumes to commission reports have often constituted compendiums of important studies, information, and syntheses of previous research. Such contributions warrant more extensive use of such commissions.

Setting research agendas and conducting research about major problems need to be closely interwoven. We therefore advocate strengthening the ability of the research community to undertaken major research programs directed toward problem exploration and to join with policy makers and research administrators in planning future research.

1.4 We recommend the support of several new research programs to undertake knowledge production and application activities to explore major social problems. Such programs will require the substantial and continuing involvement of federal policy makers and research administrators and, where appropriate, potential users of research outside the federal government. A significant level of support should be guaranteed for a period of 5 to 10 years.

For problems in areas such as education or health care delivery, where responsibility is relatively centralized in the governmental structure, support should be provided by one or a consortium of mission-oriented agencies. For problems in areas such as public regulation or regional development, where responsibility is widely dispersed across the government, other means of organizing collective action must be found. In these cases, the NSF might be able to create and support problem-centered research programs. For programs launched in this way, the burden of support might progressively be shifted to one or a consortium of mission agencies with related program interests. Congress and OMB should play an active role in maintaining consortium sponsorship as well as in monitoring the activities of research programs that are not the responsibility of a single agency.

Federal efforts to develop coordinated programs of research about particular social problems should, wherever possible, capitalize on existing research facilities, where talented staffs of applied researchers have been assembled and where strong entrepreneurial capabilities have been developed. For problem areas that do not have well-established organizational bases, new programs should be created. Federal support for 5 to 10 years will allow productive and responsive relationships to develop between researchers and potential users. We do not recommend, however, that problem-centered programs of research receive federal support for indefinite periods of time.

We wish to note that the creation of such programs need not increase the total amount of federal expenditures for social knowledge production and application. Our analysis of existing expenditures indicates that mission agencies are now devoting substantial resources to a very large number of small, poorly motivated, and largely noncumulative studies of social problems. The cost of more ambitious and cumulative programs of research could therefore be offset by selective transfers of resources from the existing investment in problem exploration.

The need to build effective research agendas on future problems is especially clear. The pace of change in our society makes it increasingly important to try to identify the problems that will need to be dealt with in future years. Since a number of such problems will at best have a loose fit with a structure of government agencies that has grown up around current and past problems, this effort may be seen as a special case of the need to deal more effectively with problems that fall between agency missions.

Of particular interest are problems with a high technological or scientific content. It is clear, for example, that future improvements in weather modification will create some critical legal, economic, and political problems, just as improved forecasting of earthquakes will create some critical economic, political, and psychological issues.

1.5 We recommend that appropriate oversight agencies foster the development of more adequate methods of forecasting emerging social problems, of defining research agendas, and of laying an adequate research-based understanding of such problems. This should include attention to the social aspect of emerging problems with a high technological or scientific content.

Among oversight agencies, the Office of Science and Technology Policy has a natural role in this area. There are also important new initiatives in Congress to deal more systematically with future needs and problems. Among independent research agencies, NSF should be encouraged to pursue the question of how society can know what it will need to know about emerging social problems.

We emphasize that what is required is not simply the ability to forecast an emerging problem. In many ways, the most critical need is to translate such forecasts into research agendas that will provide policy options in future years. The example of energy is telling. Those who analyzed the world supply of oil were able to anticipate the coming shortage. But this recognition was not translated into a program of studies that could contribute to the development of social and economic policies an era of shortage would require.

Agendas for Knowledge-Building Activities

A key issue facing independent research agencies in recent years, especially NSF, is how much criteria of relevance or social utility should complement scientific criteria in setting priorities for knowledge-building activities.

1.6 Within programs of research that seek to enlarge general resources of knowledge or method, we recommend that scientific criteria, rather than problem or policy relevance, guide the allocation of support to particular projects. The primary importance of scientific criteria should be recognized by Congress and other oversight agencies.

It is extremely difficult to predict the impact that a basic research project may have on future social policies or programs. The return on investments in knowledge building is in any case likely to depend on the cumulation of results from a number of individual projects. Premature insistence on timeliness and applicability can easily impair scientific quality. And since the ultimate applications, at the end of the long and multiple loops of knowledge-building activities, are difficult to foresee, there can be little question of user involvement in setting these research agendas. Planning should be the shared responsibility of the research community and research administrators in the research agencies, such as NSF, that support fundamental knowledge building.

The authorization and appropriation committees of Congress, and other oversight agencies, should recognize the need for including the support of basic advances of knowledge in the nation's portfolio of investments in social research and development. NSF and other research agencies should state the logic of its inclusion in clear terms. But these agencies should also take the lead in assessing the potential application of cumulating knowledge about social problems. They should have the full cooperation of the research community both in making the case for the support of basic advances of knowledge and in periodically assessing the relevance of new knowledge to social problems.

Audience

It is clear that a sharper sense of audience should guide the planning of research that is meant to benefit nonfederal users.

1.7 We recommend that agencies funding research directed to users outside the government should more effectively involve those users in setting research agendas and in developing strategies for applying research results. They should be strongly encouraged in this by the Office of Management and Budget and by Congress. We recommend further that a special review be undertaken of the effectiveness of third-party research in meeting the needs of its potential users.

A great deal more about the gap between need and benefit of federally supported work would be heard if federal expenditures for research on behalf of state and local governments approached the scale of expenditures for operating programs in which the state and local governments deliver social services that are funded by the federal government. It would be natural for the Office of Science and Technology Policy, in consultation with the Intergovernmental Science, Engineering, and Technology Advisory Panel (ISETAP), to take the lead in commissioning a review of third-party research.

DISSEMINATING AND APPLYING RESULTS

We have noted the variety of audiences to whom the results of federally supported knowledge production activities might be relevant, including federal, state, and local policy makers, program officials, field practitioners, and other researchers. There is little reason to believe that information will be received and used in the same way by each of them. If knowledge is to influence the policies, programs, and practices that are implemented to cope with social problems, it must be presented to potential users in forms that are appropriate to their needs.

We emphasize our strong belief that the key to the dissemination and use of research intended to aid in program support and policy formation is the close coordination of research planning with program and policy planning. A "demand-pull" model of use, with policy makers and program managers calling for the information they need, is much likelier to succeed than is a "supply-push" model, with research administrators trying to hawk the results of work they have supported. This should be better documented and better understood by policy makers and program officials.

2.1 We recommend that departmental and agency budget officials, the Office of Management and Budget, and congressional committees responsible for proposing agency authorizations require that more attention be given to the dissemination of high-quality research results to potential users.

We do not advocate blanket increases of agency appropriations for dissemination, but we believe that the return on federal investments in social knowledge production and application would often be enhanced if the support of dissemination were proportionately increased. For the results of knowledge-building research, academic journals provide a natural channel of dissemination and communication with other researchers. When the results of other kinds of research are available, other and perhaps more costly methods of dissemination must be used, and responsibility may fall more heavily on either performers or the funding agency. For example, policy formulation demonstrations may become policy implementation demonstrations if they generate positive results concerning impact and feasibility. Either the same or different performers may undertake the effort, but additional funds would be required.

The effectiveness of dissemination activities could be enhanced by experimental efforts to develop new ways of communicating the results of research to particular audiences. More encouragement should be given to publications, conferences, workshops, technical assistance, and the use of communications technology. Innovations such as *Evaluation* magazine, developed by NIMH to communicate new ideas and practices to administrators of mental health service organizations, have been particularly successful.

2.2 We recommend that federal agencies supporting knowledge production and application sponsor or produce on a regular, periodic basis syntheses of the knowledge gained from their research programs. Oversight institutions, particularly the Office of Management and Budget and the congressional support agencies, and perhaps the

National Science Foundation, should sponsor on a regular and periodic basis syntheses of existing knowledge concerning specific social problems or policy areas.

The results of individual research projects may have little immediate relevance to policy makers. The information useful to the policy community is often the cumulative result of many individual theoretical, methodological, and empirical investigations. Research administrators should seek more effective ways of synthesizing research findings in their program areas. In instances where program areas overlap, joint efforts may be appropriate.

Synthesis should also be a regular responsibility of oversight institutions whose jurisdictions cut across agency lines and of independent research agencies such as NSF. By supporting or producing state-of-the-art reviews, they could cumulate and synthesize knowledge that would help to define social problems that will require future policy or program action. An excellent example of such a review is the synthesis of knowledge on development in early childhood sponsored several years ago by the Office of the Assistant Secretary for Planning and Evaluation within HEW.

The understanding of the process of dissemination and use and of the role of new information in the process of innovation and change is regrettably weak. Strengthening it should be an important goal of federal investment in the creation and use of knowledge of social problems.

2.3 We recommend that more studies of the process of social change and the adoption of innovations by federal and nonfederal policy makers be conducted by agencies that support social knowledge production and application activities for those audiences. More and better information is needed about how knowledge from social research is translated into social policy or programs.

MANAGING THE SYSTEM

Our recommendations on management, broadly conceived, tend to apply to both the production and application of knowledge of social problems. Each of the recommended improvements also depends on actions both by those who have oversight of the system and by those who administer it in the funding agencies. We believe the system of federal support would be better managed if improvements were adopted in allocating resources; in the role of knowledge brokers; in the instruments of support; and in the evaluation of support programs.

Resource Allocation

We first consider possible improvements involving the allocation of resources.

3.1 We recommend that the Office of Management and Budget, the Senate and House Budget Committees (or the Congressional Budget Office at their direction), and the planning offices of federal agencies regularly review and assess the allocation of social knowledge production and application resources among policy areas, organizations, and categories of activity within their jurisdictions. These institutions should devote more effort to creating a comprehensive and comprehensible view of federally supported social knowledge production and application, so that resource allocations will be more in keeping with federal policy priorities and the capabilities of the research community.

The type of assessment we recommend is represented by the survey and analysis of budget obligations summarized in Chapter 2. This survey provides a good deal of information about federally supported social knowledge production and application activities. But an analysis, at least in the present stage, may be valuable more for the questions it poses than the answers it gives. For example, do the allocations among policy areas shown in Table 2, or the allocations among categories of activity shown in Table 1, appear reasonable to Congress, to oversight offices in the executive branch, and to the research community? Are third-party interests too heavily or not heavily enough represented? Are sufficient resources being committed to income security and employment research relative to health research? Is the large investment in statistics justified by the results? If refined and extended, such an analysis could provide the basis for a more informed matching of resources to information needs.

3.2 We recommend that the Office of Management and Budget, congressional committees, and departmental budget and planning offices periodically review the staffing and funding of agencies that support knowledge production and application with the objective of tailoring their capabilities to their missions and responsibilities.

Because oversight institutions have a stake in the success of knowledge production and application activities, they should take a sympathetic and constructive approach to solving management problems that impede high-quality performance. This is especially true of planning, policy analysis, and program development offices, which have the strongest natural ties to the research community, as well as the competence to understand research management issues. Effective oversight may require more stringent regulation of performance as well as limiting budgets on occasion, so that competent staff are not stretched too thin. Moreover, it may require that organizations such as OMB and agency budget offices refrain from penalizing research offices that, out of prudent concern for quality, do not spend their budgets by the end of the fiscal year.

We recognize that urging more intervention by oversight institutions in the management of knowledge production and application may invite more controls. Our expectation, however, is that this will not õccur. Currently, controls are more apt to result from too little exposure to the problems of research administration, rather than from too much exposure.

We should again state the case for improving the ability of research administrators to say with assurance what their future budget and staff size will be. Because good research and effective research planning require time, unexpected shifts of resources, up as well as down, are very damaging. Predictability is the key. We argue the virtues not of stable funding but of being able to plan a program with some assurance of what lies ahead.

The Use of Knowledge Brokers

The inherent differences between the research and policy processes underscore the importance of the role of individuals who understand both. One of the most promising trends in federal experience in recent years is the widening role of knowledge brokers. Such brokerage can improve performance both in launching research and in applying its results. We regard the effective use of knowledge brokers as a tool of great potential in managing the system of federal support.

The successful performance of effective knowledge brokerage within federal departments and agencies depends on brokers' having a substantial institutionalized role in the decision-making process, particularly as it affects planning, analysis, and budgeting activities.

3.3 We recommend that departments and agencies organize and manage their planning and budgeting activities to provide a significant role for knowledge brokers. Such brokers should assume increased responsibility for promoting systematic policy planning and program development within federal agencies, specifically ensuring the regular involvement of potential users in setting agendas for social knowledge production and application activities.

Choosing Instruments of Support

We have noted that there is considerable flexibility in the laws and regulations that govern the use of methods of support for social knowledge production and application activities, although current practice has, in many agencies, become standard operating procedure. Administrative processes for choosing performers of research and supporting their work have become primarily regulatory in character, relying on punitive rules and regulations to thwart undesirable practices on the part of researchers, rather than providing positive inducement to effective management.

The choice of instruments of support—whether grants, contracts, or in-house research—should be a significant and conscious part of program planning. There are strong causal relationships between the management of support activities and the quality, timeliness, and applicability of research results. Rather than responding mechanically to rigid administrative guidelines, research administrators should employ the procurement technique that is most appropriate in view of the extent to which planning, problem choice, and research design are to be shared by the support agency and the research performers.

3.4 We recommend that each agency review its grant and contract policies to increase its awareness of the options available and to match its support instruments to its research goals. We also recommend that training programs be provided, either by departmental procurement offices or by the Office of Management and Budget, to inform agency administrators and program staff concerning the uses of grants, contracts, and in-house research capabilities.

A primary reason for the unsatisfactory state of current procurement practices is that many program and research administrators are only partially informed about the possible uses of funding methods. Procurement regulations and techniques are complex. An immediate and useful step to improve relationships between funders and performers would be the wider dissemination of information about alternative methods of support.

Serious attention should also be given to improving in-house research capabilities in the federal government. The argument for this development is closely aligned to the argument for strengthening the role of knowledge brokers. Although some policy makers apply a discount to the quality and standing of in-house research personnel, the presence of these personnel may promote an easier exchange of information between policy makers who need to learn more about the implications of research and researchers who need to know more about the needs and interests of policy and program officials.

Evaluation of Support Programs

We come finally to evaluation of social knowledge production and application as a means of managing and improving the system of federal support.

3.5 We recommend that departmental planning, policy analysis, and evaluation offices promote and coordinate periodic, in-depth, and objective evaluations of the work funded by major support agencies. These evaluations should be undertaken every 5 to 10 years with priority given to the largest and most important programs. The evaluations should address the quality, timeliness, and applicability or value of the results; the appropriateness of the methods used to develop a research agenda, to choose and support performers, and to oversee the preparation, presentation, and dissemination of findings; and the relevance of the overall program to emerging social problems, scientific developments, and public policy issues. Along with departmental officials, the Office of Management and Budget should play a primary role in creating incentives for such evaluations.

Although we would also encourage self-evaluations by agencies supporting social knowledge production and application activities, such efforts are frequently subject to the criticism that they are self-serving. Sponsorship by appropriate oversight offices will enhance the credibility of evaluation results. To further ensure objectivity, such evaluations should be conducted under the auspices of an advisory committee composed in part of prominent researchers and consumers of research outside the federal government. The actual evaluation should be conducted by an outside firm or institute. Appropriate budgetary resources should be allocated to such evaluations of support programs.

Appendix

TECHNICAL NOTES ON THE
SURVEY OF FEDERAL OBLIGATIONS
FOR SOCIAL KNOWLEDGE
PRODUCTION AND APPLICATION[1]

Our survey of federal "social R&D" obligations was not meant to duplicate the surveys conducted by the National Science Foundation (NSF) and the Office of Management and Budget (OMB); we instead sought to amplify and build upon the existing data in order to describe more comprehensively the activities we define as social knowledge production and application. Our budget figures differ in three major ways from the NSF and OMB data, and these differences should be kept in mind when comparing other data with ours.[2]

First, we did not use the traditional definitions of research and development. Instead, we used the seven categories of knowledge production and knowledge application activities described in Chapter 1. Some of these categories are not included in the traditional definitions of research and development, as discussed below.

Moreover, the concept of "development" is a particularly troublesome one for the classification of R&D applied to social problems; this has long been recognized by those interested in federal support of the social and behavioral sciences. The BASS report of the National Research Council and the Social Science Research Council (1969) did not confront this question directly, but instead estimated that one percent

---

[1]These notes are adapted from Abramson (1978).
[2]For R&D statistics assembled by NSF, see the annual report, *Federal Funds for Research, Development and Other Scientific Activities.* For R&D data assembled by OMB, see Special Analysis P in the *Annual Budget of the United States Government Special Analysis.*

of all development funded by the federal government was probably social. Since development is considered a nondisciplinary activity, it is impossible to say how much of the total reported to NSF and OMB as "development" is related to the social sciences.

Hence, "development" related to social problems was something of an enigma at the outset of our survey. It was clear that substantial funds were being spent on development, broadly defined, by agencies directly concerned with such problems, but little was known about the types of activities included under this rubric. For example, the Office of Education in the Department of Health, Education, and Welfare reported almost 90 percent of its total fiscal 1976 R&D obligations as "development," but we did not know what kinds of activities were being so classified—demonstrations, curriculum development, or what?

Plainly one of our major tasks was to explore the concept of development and the nature of the activities reported under this heading by agencies concerned with social problems. This exploration led us to use the framework of knowledge production and knowledge application activities, which we felt was more descriptive of the activities actually being funded by the federal government concerned with social problems.

Second, we included research on social problems carried out by investigators in disciplines other than social science and psychology. Indeed, our definition of social research emphasized the problem rather than the disciplinary knowledge or methods applied. Hence, our total for research activities is higher than the NSF total for all basic and applied research in the social sciences and psychology. Our total also includes some multidisciplinary research categorized in the various NEC (not elsewhere classified) categories by NSF, which provides the best data on federal obligations by academic discipline.

Third, we included 14 agencies that do not report any of their activities as "research" or "development" in response to the NSF survey of R&D.[3] Although these agencies do not report any R&D expenditures, some of their activities clearly fit our definition of social knowledge production and application, even if the amounts involved

[3]The 14 agencies are: Appalachian Regional Commission, Commission on Civil Rights, Equal Employment Opportunity Commission, Council of Economic Advisers, Council on Environmental Quality, Council on Wage and Price Stability, Federal Mediation and Conciliation Service, Federal Power Commission, Federal Reserve System, International Trade Commission, Interstate Commerce Commission, National Foundation on the Arts and Humanities, the National Center for Productivity and Quality of Working Life, and the Securities and Exchange Commission.

were usually small. Therefore, we have a slightly larger data base than NSF.

Because of these three major differences, our figures are not directly comparable to those of NSF or OMB. Furthermore, our total figure for social knowledge production and application should not be interpreted as a subtotal of the figures for all federal R&D reported by either NSF or OMB.

Selected results of our survey are presented in the body of this report and at the end of this Appendix; a comprehensive report of the results is published as a separate volume (Abramson 1978).

DEFINITIONS

THE CONCEPT OF ''SOCIAL''

Social R&D consists of research and development and related activities concerned with understanding and alleviating social problems. It is intended to include such activities as the production or application of knowledge concerning the behavior of individuals, groups, or institutions or the effects of policies, programs, or technologies on behavior.

As noted in Chapter 1, this definition excludes biomedical or technological development in which only minor attention is given to social or individual impacts. We would classify as social a project in which an existing technological capability is assessed for its impact on behavior but not a project primarily attempting to develop a new technology. This definition left considerable room for judgment, but it was felt to be sound by our interviewers and by agency personnel. Although the boundaries between social and nonsocial can be hazy, the issue did not loom as large as we had expected.

CATEGORIES OF SOCIAL KNOWLEDGE PRODUCTION AND APPLICATION

Knowledge Production

RESEARCH

Research is systematic, intensive study directed toward greater knowledge of understanding of the subject studied. Social research includes basic, applied, or policy research that studies either the behavior of individuals, groups, or institutions or the effects of policies, programs, or technologies on behavior.

The first part of this definition is similar to the one used by NSF and OMB, but we did not attempt to distinguish between basic, applied, and policy research. This decision was greeted with enthusiasm by the agencies. The distinction between basic and applied research is difficult in any field but seems to be particularly difficult in the social and behavioral sciences.

The total for research reported to NSF was roughly 85 percent of our own total for research. The remaining 15 percent was not reported to NSF either because the agency spending the funds does not report to NSF or because an activity had not been considered "research."

DEMONSTRATIONS FOR POLICY FORMULATION

A demonstration is a small-scale program undertaken in an operational setting for a finite period of time to test the desirability of a proposed course of action. A demonstration for policy formulation is undertaken to learn new information about the outcomes and administrative feasibility of a proposed action. Social experiments are included in this category.

This definition, developed by our staff, was quickly understood when explained to agency personnel.[4] Approximately 50 percent of our total figure for demonstrations for policy formulation was reported to NSF as "development"; 25 percent was reported as "research"; the remaining 25 percent was not reported at all. It is clear that agencies classify this type of demonstration in different ways; but with 75 percent of the activities reported as either "R" or "D," this category would be included in an "R&D" framework.

We have noted that 25 percent of all demonstrations for policy formulation were reported as research. Thus, roughly $50 million could be added to our total for research if this subset of demonstrations for policy formulation were counted as research.[5] The two types of activities are clearly combined in some agencies. Social experiments are the type of policy formulation demonstration most closely linked to research, but we chose to categorize social experiments as policy formulation demonstrations rather than research.

PROGRAM EVALUATION

Program evaluation is evaluation that seeks to systematically analyze federal programs (or their components) to determine the extent to which they have achieved their objectives. A distinguishing factor of program evaluation is that national operating programs (or their components) are evaluated for the use of agency decision makers in making

---

[4]For a more detailed discussion of demonstrations, see Hayes, "Demonstrations," *in* Glennan (1978).

[5]This would bring the total to more than $700 million for fiscal 1976.

policy or program decisions. Program evaluation is defined as a management tool; more general types of evaluation studies (activities frequently labeled evaluation research) were judged not to be oriented to management or decision making and were categorized as research.

This definition borrows heavily from the one developed by the Evaluation and Program Implementation Division of OMB.[6] The line between research and evaluation appears to be very thin in many government agencies. Because the term evaluation is very popular today, many traditional research activities are called evaluation by agencies. But when we emphasized program evaluation, the number of "evaluation" projects was reduced.

Although some agencies have activities clearly labeled "program evaluation," most do not. When activities are labeled program evaluation, they do not seem to be reported to the NSF survey of federal funds, in line with the NSF interpretation of "research," which generally excludes program evaluation.

GENERAL PURPOSE STATISTICS

General purpose statistics include either current or periodic data of general interest and use. A characteristic of general purpose statistics is that many of the specific users and uses are unknown. These statistics provide all levels of government and the private sector with information on a very broad spectrum of social, economic, and demographic topics. Statistics that are collected for the specific purpose of providing research data in a specific area of inquiry have been categorized as research.

This definition is employed by the Statistical Policy Division of OMB (Office of Management and Budget 1975). We excluded program or administrative data from our survey because they are collected as part of an agency's routine administrative and operating responsibilities.

Statistics clearly fall outside the usual definition of research and development. As we expected, we found that general purpose statistics are rarely reported to NSF as R&D. But there are several exceptions, especially longitudinal and research-oriented data collections, which are reported both to NSF as research and to OMB as statistics.

Knowledge Application

DEMONSTRATIONS FOR POLICY IMPLEMENTATION

A demonstration is a small-scale program undertaken in an operational setting for a finite period of time to test the desirability of a proposed course of action. A demonstration for

[6]See "Evaluation Management: A Background Paper," Office of Management and Budget 1975.

policy implementation is undertaken to promote the use of a particular action. This type of demonstration does not attempt to generate new information but instead attempts to apply existing knowledge.

The concept of a policy implementation demonstration was also quickly understood by agency personnel. With few exceptions, the individuals interviewed agreed with the distinction between this and policy formulation demonstrations.

More than two-thirds of our total for policy implementation demonstrations is not reported to NSF as either research or development, while close to one-third was reported as development. Plainly, this type of demonstration seems in most cases not to be considered R&D by federal agencies. Although this activity does not fit the usual definition of R&D, we felt that policy implementation demonstrations are a type of knowledge application: when federal officials decide that enough is known about a proposed course of action, they may promote its use by launching a demonstration to "show off" the concept to potential adopters.

DEVELOPMENT OF MATERIALS

The development of materials consists of the systematic use of knowledge and understanding gained from research to produce materials. Examples of such materials are educational curriculum materials or methods, testing instruments, and management or training curricula. Such materials are used in a variety of educational, training, or testing settings.

In contrast to policy implementation demonstrations, more than two-thirds of our total for this activity is reported to NSF as development. The development of materials, like research and policy formulation demonstrations, is a category that fits comfortably within the R&D framework. This is one area of social science activity that can truly be called "development," since tangible products are developed.

DISSEMINATION

Dissemination consists of activities undertaken by research managers or others to promote the application of knowledge or data resulting from social knowledge production activities. Dissemination activities include: publication and distribution of scientific and technical information resulting from social research; documentation, reference, and information services (information retrieval systems); research syntheses written for the use of practitioners and decision makers; technical assistance to practitioners to disseminate knowledge; support of conferences to disseminate information; and creation of dissemination networks and consortia.

This definition shows that we have subsumed a variety of activities under the heading of dissemination. These activities clearly fall outside the usual definition of R&D, although NSF has termed the publication and distribution of scientific and technical information (STINFO, one of the activities falling under our dissemination heading) a "related activity." Our definition of dissemination goes much beyond the smaller concept of STINFO. Hence, the funds reported to NSF as STINFO only account for a small portion of our total for dissemination activities.

More than 50 percent of our total for dissemination (nearly $165 million) is accounted for by the activities funded by the Extension Service of the Department of Agriculture. We decided after extensive interviews with personnel in the Extension Service that its activities were largely social and fit our category of technical assistance.[7] We defined technical assistance as a dissemination activity, funded or provided by the federal government, to promote knowledge application by personal contact with practitioners or decision makers. The Extension Service agent has long been held as a model of dissemination and utilization. We felt that the Extension Service should be included in our survey, although this decision markedly increased the total for dissemination activities.

Summary

Of the seven knowledge production and application categories, three—research, demonstrations for policy formulation, and development of materials—fall within the traditional definition of R&D. Thus, approximately $980 million can be called "social R&D." The four remaining categories—program evaluation, general purpose statistics, demonstrations for policy implementation, and dissemination—totaling $832 million, fall outside the usual definition of R&D but fulfill legitimate knowledge production or application functions.

The traditional concept of development seems to cover several diverse activities in the social area—policy formulation demonstrations, some policy implementation demonstrations, and the development of materials—and small portions of other activities were also categorized as development. We feel that a knowledge production and application framework provides a more descriptive and accurate portrayal of the wide variety of activities funded by the federal government for creating and using knowledge of social problems. A detailed

---

[7]The remaining activities of the Extension Service include the dissemination of scientific agricultural information and were excluded from our totals. For a longer discussion of the Extension Service's activities, see Abramson (1978).

breakdown of these activities by agency appears in Table A-1, at the end of the Appendix.

We devoted a good deal of effort to developing the policy areas presented in Chapter 2. Instead of adopting the functional categories used by OMB or NSF, we developed a somewhat different set, closer to those recently proposed by the General Accounting Office (1977) and the House Budget Committee (U.S. Congress, House 1976a), although incorporating elements of both the existing and the proposed systems. We had to decide how detailed a set of policy categories to use and adopted relatively broad categories as more appropriate for program-level data. (As described below, the Study Project survey was based on program rather than project data.)

There are many problems inherent in classifying R&D programs by policy area. Most have a primary and secondary policy focus. A related problem was the tendency of the predominant mission of an agency to color R&D classifications by policy area. Thus, R&D programs funded by the Department of Transportation tended to be categorized as "transportation" even though these programs might be partly focused on the environment or on employment patterns. Wherever possible, we allocated the total obligations of a funding program among several policy areas. Programs were frequently divided in this way.

We did not attempt to define the 12 policy areas used in the survey, but rather described each policy area by the topics or issues most likely to be included in it. We did not define a distinct policy area for "defense" since we felt that defense activities fell outside our definition of social problems. We did, however, include the Department of Defense in our survey and wherever appropriate classified under the 12 policy areas the knowledge production and application activities funded by the department.

Human Resources

HEALTH   Health was one of the two policy areas in which data were collected by subcategory. Seven subcategories were used: health education; health care delivery and services; prevention and control of health problems; mental health; substance abuse prevention and rehabilitation; food and nutrition; and miscellaneous. Biomedical research was excluded as falling outside "social R&D." The data on the health policy area, broken down by subcategory, appear in Table A-4, at the end of the Appendix.

EDUCATION   The education category included knowledge production and application activities in the following areas: preschool education (day care, etc.); elementary, secondary, and higher education; vocational and occupational education; education for the handicapped; basic research on education; educational service delivery (educational finance, school administration); adult education; and cultural affairs. Health education activities were included under health, and science education activities were included under science and technology base.

EMPLOYMENT AND TRAINING   The employment and training category included: job training and retraining programs; the delivery of training programs; employment statistics; equal employment opportunities; programs aimed at upgrading skills and increasing participation and usefulness in the labor force; pension programs; etc. Vocational education was classified under education. (The budget classification proposed by the General Accounting Office contains this category, whereas existing classification systems do not.)

SOCIAL SERVICES AND INCOME SECURITY   The social services and income security category included: the delivery of social services; rehabilitation services; legal services; research and demonstrations on target populations (children, elderly, minorities); unemployment insurance; retirement and disability insurance; public assistance and income supplements (food stamps); veterans' benefits; and the delivery of income security programs. Knowledge production and application activities on housing assistance were included under housing and community development.

Community Resources

ECONOMIC GROWTH   The economic growth category consisted primarily of general purpose economic and demographic statistics and research on fiscal, monetary, and tax policy. Research on productivity, economic development, and business and commerce was also included in this category. This is the only policy area in our classification that does not have a comparable budget function in any of the existing or proposed budget classifications.

TRANSPORTATION   The transportation category included: transportation safety; public transportation systems; transportation patterns; and the socioeconomic aspects of transportation programs and policies. The small amount of research on telecommunications policy was included in this category.

HOUSING AND COMMUNITY DEVELOPMENT The housing and community development category included a wide range of related topics: rural housing and development; disaster prevention and relief; area and regional development; housing economics and finance; housing assistance programs; community growth; land use control techniques; intergovernmental relations; and revenue sharing.

LAW ENFORCEMENT AND JUSTICE The law enforcement and justice category included: the criminal justice system (police, courts, corrections); federal law enforcement; prevention and causes of crime; drug enforcement; etc.

INTERNATIONAL AFFAIRS The international affairs policy area included: international development; foreign assistance; international relations; international trade; and arms control and disarmament. Some of the activities of the Agency for International Development (AID) were categorized under this policy area, but other AID activities were categorized under education, health, or other policy areas where appropriate.

Natural Resources

NATURAL RESOURCES AND THE ENVIRONMENT The natural resources and environment category included knowledge production and application on the social aspects of: recreational resources; conservation and land management; pollution control and abatement; environmental regulations; water resources; etc. Technological research on improving the environment was excluded.

ENERGY DEVELOPMENT AND CONSERVATION The energy development and conservation category included knowledge production and application on the social aspects of: energy conservation; regulation of energy; energy modeling; supply and demand studies; etc.

Science and Technology Base

This category consisted primarily of the science education, science policy, and the basic social science research activities of NSF. Basic social science research in other departments was also included in this category.

Table A-2 at the end of the Appendix summarizes for each policy area the obligations for our seven types of knowledge production and application activities. Table A-3 summarizes for each policy area the obligations of 44 federal departments and agencies. Although the picture given by Table A-3 is an approximate one, it does suggest the lead agency for social knowledge production and application activities in each of the 12 policy areas.

SURVEY PROCEDURES

Our survey of federal obligations for social knowledge production and application activities was conducted between April and June 1976.[8] We surveyed approximately 180 agencies and contacted over 300 individuals. Because the knowledge production and application framework was novel and potentially difficult, we felt we could not simply rely on budget data reported by the agencies themselves. Therefore, the survey was conducted by a team of nine interviewers especially hired and trained for this purpose. A member of the project staff served as director of the survey.

We were fortunate in having access to several key documents. Most agencies provided us with copies of their fiscal 1977 congressional budget justifications, and we analyzed the budget to identify programs in which social knowledge production or application activities might occur. OMB provided us access to each agency's "R&D" and "statistical" budget special analyses for fiscal 1977. NSF gave us access to agency responses to the fiscal 1977 annual survey of "Federal Funds for R&D and Other Scientific Activities." We also had the results of the 1975 Study Project survey. Hence, we already knew a great deal about each agency prior to our interviews with agency personnel.

Agency "R&D" obligations, obtained from NSF and OMB data, were used as the starting point for our survey. We analyzed such obligations to identify those that were "social" and to classify them within our social knowledge production and application framework, refining these judgments by interviews with the persons responsible for the agency's R&D submissions. We also obtained data on activities such as program evaluation and statistics that are not included in research and development figures.

The figures presented in this report are based on estimated obligations for fiscal 1976. Data were also collected on obligations for fiscal 1975 and estimates for fiscal 1977.[9] The data collected during the spring of 1976 were estimates for fiscal 1976 made during the final quarter of

[8]An earlier survey was conducted by the Study Project during summer 1974. It gave us an overall view of the terrain and provided a test of our preliminary categories. These categories were refined for the major survey.

[9]These are presented in detail in Abramson (1978).

that fiscal year. The data are thus based on obligations made during the first three quarters of the year plus estimates of fourth-quarter obligations. It was felt that fiscal 1976 data represented the most accurate and current data available. (Fiscal 1977 estimates were based on the President's fiscal 1977 budget and did not reflect later congressional actions.) Dollar figures were based on estimated obligations, not actual expenditures or budget authority.

Our survey data include dollar figures for programs and not for individual projects. We did not press our study to the level of individual projects for two reasons: first, fiscal 1976 was not yet over and all the projects for that year had not yet been selected; second, it was deemed all but impossible to collect and categorize data on all the projects funded by the federal government for three fiscal years.

The definition of program varied among agencies. But, for the most part, a "program" represented a collection of projects in a given area. In the spring of 1976, there was a fairly accurate estimate of what each program's final obligations would be for that fiscal year. Following the conventions of OMB and NSF, "overhead" or "S&E" (salaries and expenses) was included in the data collected on each program.

TABLE A-1 Funding Patterns: Social Knowledge Production and Application by Department or Agency (fiscal 1976 obligations, $ millions)

Department or Agency	Knowledge Production Activities					Knowledge Application Activities				TOTAL
	Research	Policy Formulation Demonstrations	Program Evaluation	General Purpose Statistics	Total	Policy Implementation Demonstrations	Development of Materials	Dissemination	Total	
Department of Agriculture										
Agricultural Marketing Service			*	10	11			1	1	12
Agricultural Research Service	2				2					2
Cooperative State Research Service	25				25					25
Economic Research Service	25		2		25			6	6	31
Extension Service	1		1		2			166	166	168
Farmer Cooperative Service	1	*		*	1		*	1	1	2
Food and Nutrition Service		*		*	2		*	*	1	3
Forest Service	6		*	*	6		*	2	2	8
Soil Conservation Service	*		*	*	*			*	*	*
Statistical Reporting Service	2			29	31			*	*	31
Other agencies[a]	*	*	*	*	*			*	*	*
Total	62	*	3	41	106		1	176	177	282
Department of Commerce										
Bureau of the Census	1			65	65			1	1	66
Bureau of Economic Analysis	2			8	10			2	2	12
Domestic and International Business Administration	3			4	7					7
Economic Development Administration	9		1	*	10			3	3	13

97

TABLE A-1 (Continued)

Department or Agency	Knowledge Production Activities					Knowledge Application Activities				TOTAL
	Research	Policy Formulation Demonstrations	Program Evaluation	General Purpose Statistics	Total	Policy Implementation Demonstrations	Development of Materials	Dissemination	Total	
Maritime Administration	1				1					1
National Bureau of Standards	1	3	*		4	*			*	4
National Fire Prevention and Control Administration	*			*	*	*	*	*	1	1
National Oceanic and Atmospheric Administration	5				5					5
Office of Minority Business Enterprise	*	1			1	1			1	2
Office of Telecommunications			*	*	*			2	2	2
U.S. Travel Service	*		*		1					1
Total	22	4	2	77	106	1	*	7	8	114
Department of Defense										
Department of the Air Force	4				4		6	*	6	10
Department of the Army	17	*	*	2	19		4	1	4	23
Department of the Navy	10	*			11		3		3	14
Civil Preparedness Agency	1				1		*		*	1
Defense Advanced Research Projects	5	2			7					7
Office of the Secretary	3				3					3
Total	40	2	*	2	45		13	1	14	58

Department of Health, Education, and Welfare								
Alcohol, Drug Abuse, and Mental Health Administration								
National Institute on Alcohol Abuse	12			12		*	1	1	13
National Institute on Drug Abuse	19	17		38	1	1	3	4	42
National Institute of Mental Health	28			29	*	1	2	2	30
Total	59	17		78	1		6	7	85
Assistant Secretary for Education								
Fund for Improvement of Postsecondary Education	1	*		1			*	5	6
National Center for Education Statistics	6			10	4	4			10
Office of Assistant Secretary for Education	1			1					1
Total	8	*		12	4	4	*	5	17
Assistant Secretary for Health	2			2					2
Assistant Secretary for Planning and Evaluation	11	18	5	34					34
Center for Disease Control								
Bureau of Health Education	*	1		1	*	1	*	1	3
National Institute for Occupational Safety and Health	1			2			**	*	2
Total	1	1		3	*	1	**	1	4

99

TABLE A-1 (Continued)

Department or Agency	Knowledge Production Activities					Knowledge Application Activities				TOTAL
	Research	Policy Formulation Demonstrations	Program Evaluation	General Purpose Statistics	Total	Policy Implementation Demonstrations	Development of Materials	Dissemination	Total	
Food and Drug Administration										
Bureau of Drugs	*				*		*	*	*	1
Bureau of Foods	2	*			2			*	*	3
Other agencies b		*	1		1		1	1	1	2
Total	3	*	1		4		1	1	2	6
Health Resources Administration										
Bureau of Health Manpower	2	*			2	8	1	*	9	11
Bureau of Health Planning and Resource Development	1				1		*	3	3	4
National Center for Health Services Research	20	4	1	*	25		*	*	*	25
National Center for Health Statistics		*		26	26					26
Office of Planning, Evaluation and Legislation	1		1		1		1			1
Total	23	4	2	26	55	8	1	3	13	67
Health Services Administration										
Bureau of Community Health Services	8	1	2		11	27	*	3	30	41
Bureau of Medical Services	7	*	*		8	*	*	*	*	8

100

Indian Health Service	*		*			1	1
Office of Planning, Evaluation and Legislation		2	2		2		2
Total	15	3	21		3	31	52
National Institutes of Education							
Basic Skills Group	6	2	8	11		11	18
Dissemination and Resources Group	*	*	*		10	10	11
Education and Work Group	2	11	12	1		1	14
Educational Equity Group	8	*	8	3		3	11
Finance and Productivity Group	4	8	13			3	15
School Capacity for Problem Solving	1	2	3	1		1	4
Other[c]	1	1	1	1			1
Total	22	24	46	15	10	28	74
National Institutes of Health							
National Cancer Institute	12	5	17		*	1	19
National Heart and Lung Institute	2	2	4	1	2	3	8
National Institute of Child Health and Development	10		10		*	*	10
National Institute of Environmental Health Sciences	1		1				1
National Institute of Neurological and Communicative Disorders	3		3	1	*	*	4
National Library of Medicine	1		1	1	17	17	19

TABLE A-1 (Continued)

Department or Agency	Knowledge Production Activities					Knowledge Application Activities				TOTAL
	Research	Policy Formulation Demonstrations	Program Evaluation	General Purpose Statistics	Total	Policy Implementation Demonstrations	Development of Materials	Dissemination	Total	
Other[d]	4				4			*	*	4
Total	35	7	1		42	1	2	19	22	64
Office of Education										
Bureau for Education for the Handicapped	8	20			28	18	4	4	26	54
Bureau of Occupational and Adult Education	5	18	3		25	9	4	*	14	39
Bureau of Postsecondary Education	1	1			2		3	*	3	5
Bureau of School Systems	*	12	*		12	45	9	1	55	67
Office of the Commissioner		2	1		3	5	13	6	24	27
Office of Indian Education		5			5		1	1	1	6
Office of Planning, Budget, and Evaluation	1		13		14			1	1	15
Total	15	57	17		89	77	34	13	124	213
Office of Human Development										
Administration on Aging	6	5	2		12	7			7	19
Developmental Disabilities Office	2	1	1		3		*		*	4
Office of Child Development	15	8	3	2	29	5	1	6	12	41

	Col1	Col2	Col3	Col4	Col5	Col6	Col7	Col8	Col9	Col10
Office of Youth Development	1				1					1
Rehabilitation Services Administration	7	2	1		10	*	*	1	2	12
Total	30	16	6	2	55	12	2	7	21	76
Social and Rehabilitation Service	3	2	2		7	2			2	9
Social Security Administration	16	9			25			1	1	26
Total—Department of Health, Education, and Welfare	243	155	38	37	474	130	62	64	256	729
Department of Housing and Urban Development	10	19	4	11	44	7	3	5	14	58
Department of the Interior										
Bureau of Indian Affairs	*			*	1	*	1		1	2
Bureau of Land Management				*	2					2
Mining Enforcement and Safety Administration				1	1					1
National Park Service	4			*	4		*	*	*	4
Office of Water Research and Technology	2	2		1	2			*	*	2
Other^e	1	1	*	2	2			*	*	2
Total	9	1	1	1	12	*	1	1	1	13
Department of Justice										
Bureau of Prisons	1									1
Drug Enforcement Administration				1						1

TABLE A-1 (Continued)

Department or Agency	Knowledge Production Activities					Knowledge Application Activities				TOTAL
	Research	Policy Formulation Demonstrations	Program Evaluation	General Purpose Statistics	Total	Policy Implementation Demonstrations	Development of Materials	Dissemination	Total	
Federal Bureau of Investigation				3	3					3
Immigration and Naturalization Service	1				1					1
Law Enforcement Assistance Administration^f	26	*	5	10	41	12		6	18	58
Departmental Activities^g	1	*			1					1
Total	28	*	5	13	47	12		6	18	65
Department of Labor										
Bureau of International Labor Affairs	1		*		1					1
Bureau of Labor Statistics	1			55	56					56
Employment Standards Administration	5		*	*	6					6
Employment and Training Administration	6	3	1	7	15	2	*	1	3	18
Labor Management Services Administration	3				3					3
Occupational Safety and Health Administration	3	1	*	6	10		6	6	12	21
Office of the Secretary	1				1					1
Total	19	3	2	68	92	2	6	7	15	107

Department of State									
Agency for International Development	13	1	1	16	1	*	6	7	22
Departmental Activities^h	1		1	1	*	*	*	*	2
Total	14	1	2	17	1	*	6	7	24
Department of Transportation									
Federal Aviation Administration	5			5		1		1	6
Federal Highway Administration	8		*	8			2	2	10
Federal Railroad Administration	5	*	3	9					9
National Highway Traffic Safety Administration	6	3	8	17	6	4	1	10	27
Office of the Secretary	13	3	7	20	*	*	3	4	24
U.S. Coast Guard	1		*	1		*		*	1
Urban Mass Transportation Administration	5	1	3	14	4	2	4	10	24
Total	43	9	21	74	10	8	10	27	101
Department of the Treasury									
Internal Revenue Service	4		11	15					15
U.S. Customs Service			3	3					3
Departmental Activities^i	7			7					7
Total	11		15	25					25
ACTION	*			1					1
Advisory Commission on Intergovernmental Relations	1		*	1		*	*	*	1

TABLE A-1 (Continued)

Department or Agency	Knowledge Production Activities					Knowledge Application Activities				TOTAL
	Research	Policy Formulation Demonstrations	Program Evaluation	General Purpose Statistics	Total	Policy Implementation Demonstrations	Development of Materials	Dissemination	Total	
Appalachian Regional Commission	1	4			5	8			8	13
Civil Aeronautics Board	*				*					*
Civil Service Commission	2		*	1	3	2	1		3	6
Commission on Civil Rights	5				5			2	2	7
Community Services Administration	2	1			3	5			5	8
Consumer Product Safety Administration	2				2					2
Energy Research and Development Administration	12				12					12
Environmental Protection Agency	12		1		13					13
Equal Employment Opportunity Commission	*	*	*	1	2			1	1	3
Executive Office of the President										
Council of Economic Advisors	1				1					1
Council on Environmental Quality								1	1	1
Council on Wage and Price Stability	1				1					1
Office of Telecommunications	2	*	*		2			*	*	2
Total	4	*	*		4			1	1	6

Federal Communications Commission	1		1		*	*	1
Federal Energy Administration	5		5			*	5
Federal Home Loan Bank Board	1		1				1
Federal Mediation and Conciliation Service	*	*	*			*	*
Federal Power Commission	3	3	3				3
Federal Reserve System	6		9				9
Federal Trade Commission	2		2				2
General Services Administration	*	*	*		1	1	*
International Trade Commission	3		3				4
Interstate Commerce Commission	2		2				2
National Center for Productivity and Quality of Working Life	*	*	*		*	*	*
National Foundation on the Arts and the Humanities	1	*	1	14	3	18	18
National Science Foundation	*		*	13	*	*	*
Astronomical, Atmospheric, Earth, and Ocean Sciences	35		35				35
Biological, Behavioral, and Social Sciences	2	2	4	13	13	15	19
Science Education	28		28	3		2	30
Research Applications							
Scientific, Technological, and International Affairs	10	1	12				12
Total	76	1	80	3	13	17	97

107

TABLE A-1 (Continued)

Department or Agency	Knowledge Production Activities					Knowledge Application Activities				TOTAL
	Research	Policy Formulation Demonstrations	Program Evaluation	General Purpose Statistics	Total	Policy Implementation Demonstrations	Development ment of Materials	Dissemination	Total	
Nuclear Regulatory Commission	1				1					1
Securities and Exchange Commission	*				*					*
Small Business Administration	1	*	*		1					1
Smithsonian Institution	8	*	*		8		*	1	1	10
Tennessee Valley Authority						1		1	2	2
U.S. Information Agency	*		*		*					1
U.S. Arms Control and Disarmament Agency	*				*					*
Veterans Administration	2	2	*	1	5	2			2	7
TOTAL	655	204	61	294	1,215	183	121	293	598	1,813

Numbers may not total due to rounding.

a Agricultural Stabilization and Conservation Service; Farmers Home Administration; Rural Development Service; Rural Electrification Service.

b Bureau of Radiological Health; Bureau of Biologics; miscellaneous FDA bureaus.

c Director's Reserve; Labs and Centers; Office of Planning, Budget, and Program Analysis.

d National Institute of Arthritis and Metabolism; National Institute of Allergy and Infectious Disease; National Institute of General Medical Services; National Institute on Aging; National Eye Institute; Office of Research Resources; Fogarty International Center; National Institute of Dental Research; Office of the Director.

e Bureau of Reclamation; Office of Mineral Policy Research and Development; Bureau of Outdoor Recreation; U.S. Fish and Wildlife Service.

f National Institute of Juvenile Justice; National Institute of Law Enforcement and Criminal Justice; Office of Juvenile Justice; National Criminal Justice Information and Statistics Service.

g Office of Policy and Planning; Board of Parole.

h Office of External Research; Bureau of Educational and Cultural Affairs.

i Office of the Secretary (includes Office of Financial Analysis; Office of Research and Analysis; Office of the Assistant Secretary for Energy Policy; Office of Industrial Economics; Office of Tax Analysis; Office of Equal Employment Programs and Bank Compliance).

*Less than $0.5 million.

TABLE A-2 Funding Patterns: Social Knowledge Production and Application Activities by Policy Area (fiscal 1976 obligations, $ millions)

Policy Area	Knowledge Production Activities										Knowledge Application Activities								Total	
	Research		Policy Formulation Demonstrations		Program Evaluation		General Purpose Statistics		Total		Policy Implementation Demonstrations		Development of Materials		Dissemination		Total			
	$	%	$	%	$	%	$	%	$	%	$	%	$	%	$	%	$	%	$	%
Human resources																				
Health	164	38	50	12	11	3	39	9	265	61	43	10	12	3	116	27	171	39	436	100
Education	51	13	82	21	19	5	4	1	156	40	87	22	69	18	81	21	237	60	394	100
Employment and training	47	34	6	4	2	1	63	46	118	85	5	3	14	10	2	2	21	15	139	100
Income security and social services	49	43	28	25	13	11	3	3	92	82	10	9	2	2	8	8	21	18	112	100
Total	311	29	166	15	45	4	109	10	631	58	146	14	98	9	207	19	450	42	1,081	100
Community resources																				
Economic growth	77	37	6	3	3	2	92	45	178	86	1	1	–	–	28	13	29	14	206	100
Housing and community development	27	26	19	18	4	4	11	11	62	58	13	12	3	3	29	28	45	42	106	100
Transportation	51	45	9	8	2	2	22	20	84	74	10	9	8	7	11	10	29	26	114	100
Law enforcement and justice	29	43	*	1	5	7	13	21	47	72	12	18	–	–	6	10	18	28	65	100
International affairs	12	55	–	–	1	4	3	14	17	73	–	–	*	*	6	27	6	27	23	100
Total	196	38	35	7	14	3	143	28	387	75	36	7	10	2	81	16	127	24	514	100
Natural resources																				
Natural resources and environment	69	61	*	*	1	1	40	35	111	97	–	–	*	*	4	3	4	3	114	100
Energy development and conservation	26	89	2	6	–	–	–	–	28	95	1	2	–	–	1	3	2	5	30	100
Total	95	66	2	1	1	1	40	28	139	96	1	*	*	*	5	3	5	4	144	100
Science and technology base	54	72	2	2	1	2	1	2	58	78	2	2	13	18	1	2	16	22	74	100
TOTAL	656	36	204	11	61	3	294	16	1,215	67	183	10	121	7	293	16	598	33	1,813	100

Numbers may not total due to rounding.
*Less than $0.5 million or 0.5 percent.

109

TABLE A-3 Funding Patterns: Policy Area by Department or Agency (fiscal 1976 obligations, $ millions)

Department or Agency	Human Resources					Community Resources						Natural Resources			Science and Technology Base	TOTAL
	Health	Education	Employment and Training	Income Security and Social Services	Total	Economic Growth	Housing and Community Development	Transportation	Law Enforcement and Justice	International Affairs	Total	Natural Resources and Environment	Energy Development and Conservation	Total		
Department of Agriculture	74	55	—	3	131	45	26	—	—	8	79	72	—	72	—	282
Department of Commerce	1	*	—	—	1	106	1	2	—	—	107	5	*	5	—	114
Department of Defense	1	—	42	—	43	—	1	2	—	2	5	8	2	10	—	58
Department of Health, Education, and Welfare	310	306	1	103	721	5	2	*	*	—	7	—	—	—	1	729
Department of Housing and Urban Development	1	1	*	*	1	—	55	—	*	—	56	1	*	1	—	58
Department of the Interior	1	1	*	—	3	1	1	—	—	—	2	6	2	9	*	13
Department of Justice	—	—	—	—	—	—	—	—	65	—	65	—	—	—	—	65
Department of Labor	19	—	86	—	105	1	—	—	—	1	2	—	—	—	—	107
Department of State	13	2	—	—	16	—	1	—	—	2	3	4	—	4	1	24
Department of Transportation	—	—	—	—	—	—	—	101	—	—	101	—	—	—	—	101
Department of the Treasury	—	—	*	*	*	19	—	—	—	6	25	—	1	1	—	25
ACTION	—	—	—	1	1	—	—	—	—	—	—	—	—	—	—	1
Advisory Commission on Intergovernmental Relations	—	—	—	—	—	*	1	—	—	—	1	—	—	—	—	1
Appalachian Regional Commission	3	2	—	—	5	2	2	1	—	—	5	—	2	2	—	13
Civil Aeronautics Board	—	—	—	—	—	—	—	*	—	—	*	—	*	*	—	*
Civil Service Commission	—	—	6	—	6	—	—	—	—	—	—	—	—	—	—	6
Commission on Civil Rights	1	5	—	—	6	—	1	—	—	—	1	—	—	—	—	7
Community Services Administration	—	—	—	6	6	2	—	—	—	—	2	—	—	—	—	8
Consumer Product Safety Administration	2	—	—	—	2	—	—	—	—	—	—	—	—	—	—	2
Energy Research and Development Administration	—	—	—	—	—	—	—	—	—	—	—	—	12	12	—	12

	436	394	139	112	1,081	206	106	114	65	23	514	114	30	144	74	1,813
Environmental Protection Agency	–	–	–	–	–	–	–	–	–	–	–	–	–	13	–	13
Equal Employment Opportunity Commission	–	–	–	–	–	–	–	–	–	–	–	–	–	–	–	3
Executive Office of the President	–	3	–	–	3	2	–	–	–	–	4	1	1	1	–	6
Federal Communications Commission	–	–	–	–	–	2	1	–	–	–	1	–	–	1	–	1
Federal Energy Administration	–	–	–	–	–	–	–	–	–	–	–	5	5	5	–	5
Federal Home Loan Bank Board	–	–	–	–	1	1	–	–	–	–	1	–	–	–	–	1
Federal Mediation and Conciliation Service	–	*	–	–	*	–	–	–	–	–	–	–	3	3	–	*
Federal Power Commission	–	–	–	–	–	9	–	–	–	–	9	–	3	3	–	3
Federal Reserve System	–	–	–	–	9	2	–	–	–	–	2	–	–	–	–	9
Federal Trade Commission	–	–	–	–	2	–	*	–	–	–	*	–	–	–	–	2
General Services Administration	–	–	–	–	–	–	–	–	–	–	4	–	–	–	–	*
International Trade Commission	–	–	–	–	2	2	–	2	–	–	4	–	–	–	–	4
Interstate Commerce Commission	–	–	–	–	–	–	–	–	–	–	2	–	–	–	–	2
National Center for Productivity and the Quality of Working Life	–	–	–	–	*	*	–	–	–	–	*	–	–	–	–	*
National Foundation on the Arts and the Humanities	18	18	–	–	18	8	8	2	–	–	18	3	1	4	–	18
National Science Foundation	2	–	5	5	7	7	8	2	–	–	*	3	1	1	67	97
Nuclear Regulatory Commission	–	–	–	–	–	–	–	–	–	–	–	–	1	–	–	1
Securities and Exchange Commission	–	–	–	–	–	–	–	–	–	–	1	1	–	–	–	*
Small Business Administration	–	–	–	–	1	1	–	–	–	–	–	1	–	1	–	1
Smithsonian Institution	–	3	–	3	3	–	2	–	–	–	2	1	–	1	5	10
Tennessee Valley Authority	–	–	–	–	–	–	–	–	–	–	1	–	–	–	–	2
U.S. Information Agency	–	–	–	–	–	–	–	–	–	1	–	–	–	–	–	1
U.S. Arms Control and Disarmament Agency	–	*	*	*	–	*	–	–	–	*	*	–	–	–	–	*
Veterans Administration	6	–	–	–	7	–	–	–	–	–	*	–	–	–	–	7
TOTAL	436	394	139	112	1,081	206	106	114	65	23	514	114	30	144	74	1,813

*Less than $0.5 million.

111

TABLE A-4 Funding Patterns: Social Knowledge Production and Application Activities by Categories of the Health Policy Area (fiscal 1976 obligations, $ millions)

Categories of the Health Policy Area	Knowledge Production Activities										Knowledge Application Activities								TOTAL	
	Research		Policy Formulation Demonstrations		Program Evaluation		General Purpose Statistics		Total		Policy Implementation Demonstrations		Development of Materials		Dissemination		Total			
	$	%	$	%	$	%	$	%	$	%	$	%	$	%	$	%	$	%	$	%
Health education	5	20	3	12	*	1	–	–	8	33	8	33	4	17	4	16	17	67	25	100
Health care delivery and services	47	31	24	16	7	5	28	19	106	71	33	23	1	*	8	6	42	29	148	100
Prevention and control of health problems	22	45	6	13	1	2	6	12	34	72	2	3	6	12	6	13	14	28	48	100
Mental health	30	92	–	–	*	1	*	1	31	95	–	–	–	–	2	5	2	5	32	100
Substance abuse prevention	31	57	17	31	1	2	1	2	50	91	–	–	1	2	4	7	5	9	55	100
Food and nutrition	1	1	–	–	*	1	*	*	1	2	–	–	–	–	72	98	72	98	74	100
Health, other	29	55	*	1	1	3	3	6	34	64	–	–	1	1	19	35	19	36	53	100
TOTAL	164	38	50	12	11	3	39	9	265	61	43	10	12	3	116	27	171	39	436	100

Numbers may not total due to rounding.
*Less than $0.5 million or 0.5 percent.

References

Abramson, M. A. (1978) *The Funding of Social Knowledge Production and Application: A Survey of Federal Agencies*. Volume 2 of the Study Project on Social Research and Development. National Research Council. Washington, D.C.: National Academy of Sciences.

Berman, P., and McLaughlin, M. W. (1974) *Federal Programs Supporting Educational Change*. Santa Monica, Calif.: RAND Corporation.

Comroe, J. H., Jr., and Dripps, R. D. (1976) Scientific basis for the support of biomedical science. *Science* 192:105-111.

George, A. L., et al. (1975) Towards a more soundly based foreign policy: making better use of information. Appendix D in volume 2 of the *Report of the Commission on the Organization of the Government for the Conduct of Foreign Policy*. Washington, D.C.: U.S. Government Printing Office.

General Accounting Office (1977) *The Need for a Government-Wide Budget Classification Structure for Federal Research and Development*. PAD-77-14 and PAD-77-14A. Washington, D.C.: General Accounting Office.

Glennan, T. K., Jr., ed. (1978) *Studies in the Management of Social R&D: Selected Issues*. Volume 4 of the Study Project on Social Research and Development. National Research Council. Washington, D.C.: National Academy of Sciences.

Lynn, L. E., Jr., ed. (1978a) *Knowledge and Policy: The Uncertain Connection*. Volume 5 of the Study Project on Social Research and Development. National Research Council. Washington, D.C.: National Academy of Sciences.

Lynn, L. E., Jr., ed. (1978b) *Studies in the Management of Social R&D: Selected Policy Areas*. Volume 3 of the Study Project on Social Research and Development. National Research Council. Washington, D.C.: National Academy of Sciences.

National Research Council (1975) *Knowledge and Policy in Manpower: A Study of the Manpower Research and Development Program in the Department of Labor*. Committee on Department of Labor Manpower Research and Development. Washington, D.C.: National Academy of Sciences.

National Research Council and Social Science Research Council (1969) *The Behavioral and Social Sciences: Outlook and Needs*. Behavioral and Social Sciences Survey Committee. Washington, D.C.: National Academy of Sciences.

Office of Management and Budget (1975) *Statistical Services of the United States Government*. Washington, D.C.: U.S. Government Printing Office.

Office of Management and Budget (1976) *Special Analysis Budget of the U.S. Government*. Washington, D.C.: U.S. Government Printing Office.

President's Commission on Federal Statistics (1971) *Federal Statistics*. 2 volumes. Washington, D.C.: U.S. Government Printing Office.

Stokes, D. E., ed. (1978) *The Uses of Basic Research: Case Studies in Social Science*. Volume 6 of the Study Project on Social Research and Development. National Research Council. Washington, D.C.: National Academy of Sciences.

U.S. Congress, House (1976a) Recommendations for improving the budget functional categories. Working paper of the House Budget Committee. *Congressional Record* (Feb. 10):H929.

U.S. Congress, House (1976b) *Statutory Provisions Related to Federal Research and Development*. 2 volumes. Committee print, Serial KK. Subcommittee on Domestic and Scientific Planning and Analysis of the Committee on Science and Technology. 94th Congress, 2nd Session. Washington, D.C.: U.S. Government Printing Office.